HOLLY FORREST is the pseudonym of an entertainment
i͟ ͟ ͟alist with more than fifteen years' experience in the
͟biz world.

HOLLY FORREST

Confessions of a Showbiz Reporter

The Friday Project
An imprint of HarperCollins
77–85 Fulham Palace Road
Hammersmith, London W6 8JB

www.harpercollins.co.uk

This edition published by The Friday Project in 2013

ISBN: 978-0-00-751773-2

Set in Minion 10.5/13.5 pt
Typeset by Palimpsest Book Production Limited, Falkirk, Stirlingshire

Printed and bound in England by
Clays Ltd, St Ives plc

Find out more about HarperCollins and the environment at
www.harpercollins.co.uk/green

As you might have heard said before a film, everything here is 'inspired by true events'. However, to protect confidentiality some names have been changed and certain elements of the stories have been fictionalised. Nonetheless, they remain an honest reflection of my experience working in showbiz journalism over many years. Enjoy!

Cyber celebrities

Top ten celebrity internet searches of 2012[1]

Kim Kardashian
Justin Bieber
Miley Cyrus
Rihanna
Lindsay Lohan
Katy Perry
Selena Gomez
Jennifer Aniston
Nicki Minaj
Taylor Swift

These ten people are basically my bread and butter.

In my time as a showbiz reporter, the biggest change I've seen is just how much we rely on these internet searches. The web might have started out as a geek's playground in the nineties, but it's now entirely mainstream – and it's my biggest outlet. I write stories that go up on it, I research celebs that I'm interviewing

[1] According to the names entered into the Bing search engine.

with it and I buy things from ASOS through it when I've got an event to attend. Like it is for many people, the internet is part of my job's daily routine.

In my line of work, though, the internet has achieved a fairly unique breakthrough: it has given *you* more power. You're my boss. True, someone needs to write features about these stars in the first place, but once they're online, it's up to you who you search for. Just look at the first two names for proof. Kim Kardashian and Justin Bieber became global brands purely through the power of the internet; fans latched on to their appeal way before us in the press. I'm not sure the people watching grainy footage of Kim getting it on with her boyfriend were the same as those watching a 12-year-old Justin singing R'n'B on YouTube, but the principle is the same. The media can still do a lot to fuel a showbiz fire, but more now than ever, what's hot is often out of our hands. With a largely free internet at our fingertips, the celebrity world is more accessible than ever before.

So after I've done my bit – writing and researching articles, interviewing celebrities, attending junkets – it's over to you. Who you spend your time looking up determines who we spend our time focusing on. If you resent that eminent scientists and liberal thinkers are missing from the list, start searching for a few and maybe we'll have to take notice. But that's the great thing about modern media: it's no longer so full of snobby journalists hiding out in their ivory towers, bleating about what they fancy and taking no notice of their audience. The internet's too transparent for that. These days, we're all in this showbiz world together.

And what a world it is . . .

Just another sunday night

Sunday 12 February 2012. It's the night of the BAFTA Film Awards ceremony and I'm bloody freezing.

We're in the heart of what we call the 'season' – those few months during which all the key awards ceremonies seem to take place, everything from the Brits to the Oscars, the BAFTAs and the Elle Style Awards. The trouble with the 'season' is that it's always during the winter. Fine, maybe, for the celebs who party until the small hours in the heated surroundings of the Royal Opera House or the O2, but for us reporters standing outside on the red carpet waiting for them to talk into our microphones, the setting is just a few degrees away from being positively arctic.

I watch my breath blossom into steam in the icy air and crack open yet another hand-warmer pad, tucking it discreetly into the back of my knickers so that it warms the small of my back. Bliss. There's the first lesson from the showbiz world for you: underneath the opulence there's always something significantly more unglamorous.

I'm huddled behind a rope with a group of fellow reporters, all women in evening dresses as per the rules of such an upmarket event. Even at an occasion like the BAFTAs, it seems odd to see people so smartly dressed packed into a small space like animals.

We'd probably look more at home in the orange suits worn by caged prisoners in Guantanamo Bay. Still, we all courteously compliment each other on our outfits, despite recognising that it's difficult to look fabulous when you're shaking harder than a nervous *X Factor* contestant.

An ice-cold wind blows up this back street of London's Covent Garden area, a road that has been transformed into something truly special, with huge spotlights, advertising banners and that all-important crimson flooring. On one side of the carpet are scores of reporters; on the other are crowds of fans. Every reporter is required to wear an all-important accreditation around our necks and be in position about an hour before the famous people actually start turning up. We've now been here about 55 minutes. The tension is palpable. So is the frost forming at the end of my nose.

. . . And then it begins, not the celebrity procession, but an unstoppable thought growing in my brain. Every time I have to cover one of these events, it's always the same. I can't help it. I'm gritting my teeth; it's still there, a loud scream in my head, shouting out in capital letters as I check my watch for the millionth time:

'I BLOODY HATE THIS JOB!'

The bubbly girl huddled next to me is someone I've only seen reporting from the red carpets for the last few months; she smiles at me and giggles. Newbies – they're the only ones that look happy.

'You okay?' she asks.

'Hmmmmm,' I mumble back.

On the outside I smile back at her. Inside I'm crying. She'll understand one day.

Then, suddenly, a roar of excitement erupts from down the line. I crank my head around to see what's happening. Someone is arriving! I rise up from my frozen slouch, microphone at the ready. The carpet is finally starting to fill, a stream of invited guests, not all famous, but each lucky enough to have a ticket to the British movie world's most important night. The screams in the distance suggest a big star has stepped out of their limousine and is beginning the long walk past the crowds. Around me I hear mumbled suggestions as to who it could be:

'Is it Clooney?'

'Please let it be Michael Fassbender!'

'Knowing our luck it'll be Peter Andre.'

The shouting is getting louder, deafening almost. Camera flashes spark out from the crowds. *Okay, Holls*, I tell myself, *here we go.* It's time to snap out of the black mood. Women with clipboards are scurrying about at the fence in front of me, talking into headsets and suddenly pointing in my direction. So much action after so much nothing. I shift the hand-warmer pad on my back slightly and take a deep breath. Then someone says . . .

'Brad, this is Holly Forrest.'

In the blink of an eye, Brad Pitt is standing in front of me. Shit! Brad ruddy Pitt! He's smirking, rubbing his hands together to keep warm and looking at me expectantly. The PR girl who's introduced him stands silently to his side. After an hour of twiddling my thumbs, I have about half-a-second to crank into gear.

'Hi,' I say. Except I don't. What I actually say is more like 'huh'. My mouth has become so frozen from the cold that my face is more like a ventriloquist's than a professional journalist.

'Oh. Hi, Holly. Are you okay?'

'Yersh, fine.'

Brad Pitt is looking at me weirdly. In an attempt to regain feeling in my lips I'm pouting like a Page 3 girl, and it's clearly got him a little worried.

'We've met before, right?'

Suddenly, my face flushes. I can feel warmth in my skin again. In fact, I'm blushing. Well, that's certainly one way of getting my facial features back into working order, I think – get a major Hollywood heart-throb to say that he remembers you. Who cares if I've just been doing ridiculous mouth acrobatics in front of one of the world's most famous men? None of that matters any more because *Brad Pitt has said that he remembers me.*

Of course, the second lesson of the showbiz world is that celebs often pretend to recognise you, because they know how great it makes you feel. Does Brad *really* remember me? I quickly calculate that I have interviewed him at least three times before so although it's unlikely, it's not actually out of the question. In truth, the warm buzz of excitement now washing over me doesn't mind whether he's lying or not. If you want to play that game, Bradley, I'll go with it.

The hour that I've been waiting here, slowly freezing and losing the will to live, begins to feel like a distant memory. Cold? What cold? The passion of the crowds, the importance of the night and the fact that I've now got Benjamin Button at his most beautiful standing just a couple of feet away and claiming to know me are all combining to remind me of something very important, something that up until a few minutes ago I'd completely forgotten. It's a feeling that always comes back. It's all I can do now to stop myself from running up the length of the red carpet in front of me and blurting it out to the crowd.

'I BLOODY LOVE THIS JOB!'

Shaking any distractions out of my head I focus and the interview begins, a well-rehearsed two-hander that Brad and I have both performed many times. Now my mouth has defrosted I'm quickly into the usual line of investigation.

'What do you think are your chances of winning?'

'What attracted you to the role?'

'How's the family?'

I know – not exactly Paxman, right? Red carpets, though, aren't the place for intensity. It's all just a show and everyone's got a script to follow. Even Brad:

'I'm just proud to be nominated . . . The role had a lot of scope to it . . . Angie and the kids are hanging at home right now . . .'

Despite the formality, I'm loving it. 'How could I *ever* complain about this job?' I'm thinking, as I occasionally lose myself in his sea-blue eyes. This is my home. The chaos going on around me as more stars arrive; the screams of fans, the hails of reporters and photographers; the antenna in my head constantly listening out for a headline or a scoop: these are my comfort zones. The third lesson in showbiz reporting is that this job has a habit of stirring up conflicting emotions, highs and lows – but ultimately I always come back to the same happy conclusion. Right now, there is no other place I'd rather be.

The beaming new girl calls over to me and I'm back down to earth. My 45 seconds with Brad has finished and he's moved on up the line.

'I saw you, Holly Forrest! You were flirting with Brad Pitt.'

'What? And you wouldn't?' I call back. It's true, though, and I'm still flushing. It's not just that I've forgotten about it being cold. I'm now actually hot under the collar.

Brad Pitt, ladies and gentlemen. When it comes to heating you up, he's significantly more effective than a hand-warmer pad down your pants.

College

I had been fascinated by showbiz for a long time, probably because I came from a very average background. The god-like looks and lifestyles of the rich and famous were far removed from my own sedate upbringing; I couldn't help but be dazzled by their tropical allure. But as a child sat gawping in front of *Top of the Pops* every Thursday night, it never occurred to me that I could make a living from the entertainment world. I was far too meek and mild a character to ever be a performer myself; that celebrities had the guts that I lacked to be in the spotlight was part of their mystique. It was only when I grew older, crucially in those final weeks of my English degree when I really needed to start thinking about how I would earn a salary, that it occurred to me that the life of a showbiz reporter could be the one for me. While I might never emulate my teen heroes – acting like Julia Roberts, singing like Mariah Carey or dancing like Paula Abdul – I could at least bask in their glow a little closer. And, who knows, by mingling with the glitterati, maybe some of their confidence would even rub off on me too? This career could be part enjoyment, part psychiatry.

How did I turn this into reality? First of all, like many career paths, I had to study, which certainly wasn't as enjoyable as I'd hoped it might be. Journalism, I was convinced, could be exciting and revolutionary; the right words, the perfect questions, could inform, entertain and even shape history. Being *taught* how to do that, however, was a strangely monotonous nuts-and-bolts experience – and, like analysing a joke, often lost sight of what made it fun in the first place.

Let's take a trip back to the late nineties, and I'll tell you all about it. Britpop's on the radio, Leo's playing Romeo at the cinema and – like every student in the country – I'm ploughing my way through cult classic *The Beach* by Alex Garland.

Oh, I can taste the pints of snakebite and black just thinking about it . . .

I was studying at a small town college in northern England. I was actually only there for a few months but, because I was miserable, it seemed like a lifetime. After my interesting and undeniably free-thinking degree in English Literature, this much more practical postgraduate course felt very dry. Suddenly, after three years of fanciful theories and intellectual posturing, I had to be straight and serious. As an undergrad, I floated about quoting Virginia Woolf and had few worries about the future. Now I was knuckling down and preparing for an actual job.

I'd enjoyed writing for the student newspaper as an undergrad and had watched every episode of *Press Gang* as a young girl; I knew what I wanted to do and was aware that some kind of professional qualifications wouldn't go amiss if I wanted to be a proper entertainment journalist. This was, after all, in the days before anyone could start up a blog and become a 'writer'. Back then wannabe journalists felt the need to actually – shock horror – train. I'd plumped for this particular course simply because it had been the only one with a flyer in my university's careers library.

This postgrad diploma, while adding another few thousand pounds to my student loan, should at least help me to fulfil my dream. By learning the ropes of writing a story and doing an interview I'd be able to then use that knowledge to focus on my chosen field of entertainment. It was a big commitment but – in my head at least – simple. I was confident I'd be joined by fellow open-minded arts students, so what could go wrong?

My peers and lecturers, of course, had other ideas. While the course I chose was no doubt a fabulous one for people wanting to be political heavyweights writing for the *Financial Times*, my showbiz goals were slightly less catered for. All traces of entertainment had seemingly been deleted from our lessons. I spent my days in shorthand classes – an utterly boring skill which teaches you, over many hours, to simply write *a little bit quicker* – and getting 'vox pops' on the streets. God I hate 'vox pops', the technical term for the soundbites journalists collect from people out doing their shopping which you see on news programmes and read in the papers ('vox pop', a rather slang Latin term, translates as 'voice of the people'). Just one glimpse of my sullen face, giant microphone in hand, and the locals would scurry away from me. Chris Brown would get a better welcome at a women's refuge. This, I would think to myself as I made my way back to college with only the wise words of the local street cleaner on my minidisc recorder, wasn't as much fun as talking about gigs, gossip and the latest happenings on *Hollyoaks*. It was going to be a long few months . . .

Getting started

Part I: My First Story

'Boyzone are outselling The Spice Girls by two to one.'

Not, I realise, a groundbreaking scoop up there with Kate Middleton topless or George Michael caught getting naughty in an LA loo (thank you to *The Sun* for their headline: 'Zip me up before you go go'). Still, the battle between the Irish crooners and girl power will always be special to me. It was my first attempt to liven up my journalism course, and my first ever showbiz story. It was the scoop that showed me the way.

On that fateful day, half-asleep after another lesson in local government, I was instructed by my tutor to head into town and simply 'find a story'. This is what, we were told, real journalists do when their publication or broadcaster is short of material. They just find out stuff and record it, like a nosey neighbour with a notebook. So, jotter in hand, I shuffled off into the streets to find a scoop. But I had a problem – if I tried to bluff my way through a chat about politics, the person I was talking to would easily catch me out. That I didn't know the first thing about NHS funding or interest rates was written on my face. But if could find an entertainment story, I would be on safe ground. My fellow students could do with a bit of frivolity too.

An hour later, the whole class was back in our makeshift news-room, preparing to share our freshly unearthed breaking news stories with our sniffy lecturer.

'The housing market in the area has seen a significant rise in the last few weeks according to a local estate agent,' said one girl, a 21-year-old like me, but with the smug air of a City banker on 200 grand a week, before snapping her notebook shut with a what-do-you-think-of-*that*? flourish.

'Very good,' replied my tutor. 'That's just the kind of thing we're hunting for. Strong, clear stuff. Who's next?'

A boy who had annoyed me from the beginning of term now piped up. Vocally religious to the point of tedium, he never wasted any opportunity to harp on about his piety.

'The priest at St Michael's is strenuously opposed to the prospect of a casino opening on the outskirts of town. I called by the church and he was more than happy to talk to me.'

'Excellent,' responded our tutor with ever-growing jollity. Our tutor was a dapper little man with an upper-class way of expression: 'A top notch story. Follow that one up please.' The Archbishop of Canterbury in front of me seemed to momentarily forget his modesty and looked extremely pleased with himself.

And then, it came. 'So . . . Holly. Over to you. What eye-opener have *you* got for us?'

Okay. Here we go. I looked down at my notes then back up at the faces staring at me. I knew they wouldn't like it. My peers were a surprising bunch, all of us were barely out of adolescence, but their earnestly worthy approaches to life were a real downer for me. Their heroes were Kate Adie and Trevor McDonald. Mine were French and Saunders.

'Boyzone are outselling The Spice Girls by two to one,' I blurted out, fully aware that this would probably go down about as well as a supermodel at a slimming club.

A couple of snorts came from the audience then a painful silence. The tutor in charge raised a quizzical eyebrow.

'And this is news because . . .?'

'W-well,' I stammered. 'This is the big pop battle of the moment. Boys versus girls. And these sales figures, well they're a sneak preview into who's going to win the fight. The guy in HMV said he wasn't even supposed to tell me but I bought the new Jamiroquai CD from him to help sweeten the pill. Midweek sales figures are a bit of a secret, you know.' (A few years later websites would proudly print the official midweek sales figures without hesitation. Back then, things were a little more surreptitious.)

Silence. I suspected that the kind of numbers I was interested in – the Top 40 broadcast on the radio every Sunday – weren't the kind he thought I should be spending my time on. That day's FTSE figures, fair enough. But new entries and highest climbers? Big mistake.

'Hmmm, I don't think so,' he replied with his military air. 'It's not really front-page stuff is it? A bit frivolous. Anyone got anything that's *proper* news?'

The Spice Girls, I don't need to remind you, went on to dominate both the music industry and the media all over the world. Everyone wanted to know about them. Posh Spice changing her hair from a bob to a pixie cut might not be as politically significant as the property market or Sunday trading, I knew that, but to suggest it's not headline-worthy nor interesting to millions of people is to underestimate the power of the entertainment world – the industry, incidentally, that is Britain's biggest export. Among my peers my interests appeared frothy, but I knew that when a star arrives that offers something fresh, something different, something exciting, millions of people want to know more. Passions are ignited and we can't get enough. Sat there, head hung low, feeling as out of place as a porn star at Disneyland, I was more determined than ever to immerse myself in this business of escapism. I would prove to these squares that it did have a point. Showbiz was an inspiration to the world and I wanted to be inspired for a living. And to inspire.

Part II: The Lucky Break

At every opportunity over the next few months I dropped a showbiz story into our daily meetings. Eyes never failed to roll, but I didn't care. I'd discovered how to enjoy myself. I kept my head down and, amid the atmosphere of collective paranoia in which my peers fought over the same job adverts in the Media section of *The Guardian* every Monday, I focused on one kind of career in one kind of place: I wanted to be a showbiz reporter in London.

It wasn't long before I came across a 'situations vacant' that suited my ambitions. The advert had explained that the editor of an entertainment magazine in the capital was looking for a junior to help cover the slew of music festivals the summer had to offer and generally assist around the office. Perfect, I thought, as I sealed the envelope containing my CV. Unsurprisingly it was an ad all my fellow students had studiously ignored. After what seemed a lifetime's wait, I got a call asking me to go for an interview with the editor. I couldn't believe it. Apparently she'd liked the chatty, friendly style of my application. It was just after Easter when I finally headed down on the train to London, ready for my moment. The questions asked about the showbiz world didn't catch me out, but I feared the awfully middle-aged green business suit I stupidly decided to wear could be my undoing. The editor sat opposite me in the boardroom, her face non-committal, her outfit effortlessly chic. I journeyed back to college that night hopeful but realistic.

The next evening I found out I'd got the job. I'D GOT THE JOB! I would start as soon as my course finished in June.

So it was, a couple of months later, that term ended and, as my fellow students headed off to write about budgets and elections in a variety of newspapers, I left small town life and headed south to the big city with only a portable TV and bag full of clothes to my name. I would be renting a studio flat on an inner city main road, sharing with my old Uni friend Erica, and earning barely £200 a week. My parents, I could tell, were petrified. But it didn't matter to me. The dream was coming true.

The rest, as they say, is history . . .

Publicists

The first people I met once I'd stepped through the doorway into the world of celebrity journalism, however, were not celebrities. They were publicists. And it wasn't long before I realised that while the showbiz world had for many years appeared to me to run effortlessly like a well-oiled machine, it's because of these publicists who are hidden away behind the cogs spraying on the WD40. In the entertainment world, talent and originality count for surprisingly little. Publicity, on the other hand, is everything. For every unrecognised genius *without* a publicist raising their profile, there's a bimbo hogging the limelight with a team pushing them into the papers.

Heading to London that June, wellies on foot, ready for three months of festival-going, I hadn't even considered there were backroom teams running the show. If you'd asked me then what a plugger was, I'd have said some kind of electrician. Now, of course, after many years in the industry, these people are a part of my life, many high on my list of best friends, others mortal enemies. It was only after making this discovery, that when watching episodes of *Absolutely Fabulous* that I totally got what the joke is. Before I laughed at the panto-like silliness of it all but now . . . Now, I *know* those characters.

Publicists are the behind-the-scenes string pullers, the reasons why you open up newspapers or log on to a website and see the same faces again and again. Just out of shot, invisible to the general public, publicists are pulling favours with the press to get their client snapped, written about or interviewed. 'Do a feature on this new up-and-comer that I've just signed up,' they might suggest, 'and I'll let you have an exclusive with my big name in a couple of months.' Their lives are a maelstrom of schedules and sweet-talking, BlackBerrys permanently attached to their hands like children clinging to their comfort blankets; their days packed with meetings over skinny lattes, their nights with more meetings over popping champagne corks. If ultimately their job is little more than a very posh take on the nightclub bouncer – 'I can't squeeze you into the interview schedule' their version of 'You're name's not down, you're not coming in' – reporters quickly come to realise that it is these super-efficient sideliners that run the show. If they say 'jump', we say 'how high?' Cross them and we won't be getting close to the big names.

This was just one aspect of show business that I had to learn fast. Plonked into the office on my first day, I was painfully aware that my new colleagues really didn't have the time to hold my hand and teach me the ropes. I'd have to learn the hard way by simply getting stuck in. So it was, after chasing a few leads handed to me by my new boss, I worked out that there are several types of publicist in the showbiz world, each slightly different to the other although all, ultimately, doing the same thing – getting their client 'out there', into the public eye.

It was with a music industry publicist – a plugger – that I had my very first dealings.

We'd just spoken on the phone and arranged, at the request of my boss, an interview with a band's guitarist who had apparently had some of his kit stolen the night before. I was to head to a studio on Holloway Road in London and speak to the unlucky performer about his recent loss. The band were nineties poster boys – complete with floppy hair and smooth-skinned good looks. 'What a great scoop!' I naïvely thought as I made my way to the venue, especially excited at doing a story on a band that I'd loved for several years.

'Just a few days into my first job and I'm already sniffing out stories!' I congratulated myself.

A lovely bloke he was too, sitting on a giant speaker in the middle of the floor of the studio, attempting to sound forlorn at the loss of his favourite Fender. We had a good chat; with me surprised to find it much easier to talk to pop stars than to real people in the street. However, while I don't doubt the robbery, the plugger had obviously seen this whole situation less as time for the band to sit around mourning and more as a great opportunity for a bit of publicity. They did, coincidentally, have a new single coming out and upcoming gigs to promote after all. Suddenly, thanks to some greedy thieves in North London, there was a 'hook' on which to get the band in the limelight again and unbeknownst to me, I'd been dragged right in. The story was mentioned on the television news that night, the band's new video getting played in the process, and *boom* maybe a few more thousand record sales as a result. So, there was my professional showbiz news debut: as a stooge in a small yet cunning piece of PR spin. And this was with a credible band in the days before reality TV and endless gossip magazines – corners of the industry that now exist on a diet of such carefully fed stories – had really kicked off.

Pluggers would prove to be a big part of my life during the coming months, as I wrote my way through a roll call of late nineties musicians to fill the magazine's pages. Some were already legends – Tom Jones, Phil Collins; others went on to have long careers – the Stereophonics and Ronan Keating, whose sales figures

I had so eagerly announced back in that classroom at college. Many are now, alas, just footnotes in the history pages of pop; hello to Chumbawamba and Kavana. All of them had their pluggers, more often than not cheeky-chappy public school boys in their thirties, who dressed and behaved as if they were 17 and from Hackney. They boasted a passive-aggressive swagger that was part seasoned music industry insider, part market trader. If their drawn faces gave away just how hard they partied you couldn't dismiss their influence. It quickly became clear that the music business was being run by frustrated rock stars.

Film publicists, though ostensibly doing the same job, are a very different breed. Like music publicists, they may have their own independent companies or they may work directly for a big label or studio. But unlike pluggers, film publicists are a mainly female race of clipboard huggers, who reek of refinement rather than roll-ups. I've often wondered if, at exclusive girls' boarding schools, there's some kind of work placement scheme within the film industry, since so many of the publicists seem to be only a few pairs of jodhpurs away from being part of the monarchy (both Sophie Rhys-Jones, aka the Countess of Wessex, and Tom Parker Bowles, stepson of Prince Charles, have worked in film and events publicity). To public school girls from the home counties, segueing into PR seems to be as natural as driving a Range Rover and holidaying at your parents' farmhouse in Provence. Their love lives might sometimes suffer (long hours are part of the job description, since so much is done 'on LA time' – i.e. the middle of the night), but what these girls lack in romance, they gain in desperate journalists wanting to be their friends.

Ultimately, I prefer to work with film publicists. With their tall, slender builds and glossy hair, they might have a habit of making my genes feel extremely average, but there's a classiness there that the pluggers seem to want to avoid. It's like comparing Jamie

Oliver to Nigella Lawson. I guess sophistication just isn't very rock 'n' roll. However, unlike pluggers, who all seem to have a real passion for music (as I said, they're frustrated pop stars), it's rare that I meet a film publicist who's a dedicated *cinéaste*. But they are very good at wearing black and organising press schedules.

Every corner of showbiz has its own publicists, not just music and movies. There are book PRs, television PRs, theatre PRs, fashion PRs and events PRs, arts PRs, the list goes on. Each breed of these fixers, pushers and spin doctors might have slightly different traits but ultimately they all share one very important thing in common: without them, I'd be screwed.

London

The late 1990s. Rush hour. And I was cycling down Oxford Street in London. Ask me to do this now and I'd laugh in your face, warned off by ten years of accident horror stories and, more importantly, the idea of cycling anywhere in the kind of outfits I usually wear. As a green and naïve newbie on the other hand? I was off and pedalling quicker than you can say 'Pendleton thighs'.

This was during my first few months as a salaried journalist at the magazine. A celebrity court case was taking place at the now-closed Bow Street Magistrates Court and I had been informed by my panicking boss late one afternoon that I needed to get down there, and fast.

'Y-y-y-you want me to report on the story?' I stuttered, wide-eyed and in shock.

'Don't be silly, Holly –' She smiled at me in that kind but patronising way bosses are so good at '– Sophie's down there and the batteries have run out on her recorder. I need you to get down there bloody quickly with these.' She opened up her palm in front of me to reveal a four pack of Duracell.

Yes, my life was sooo glamorous.

'Dappy cow should've taken spares obviously but there you go. If she's not up and running in the next half an hour, she'll miss the post-verdict statement on the steps. With shorthand as bad as hers, I can't rely on her getting anything down. Take my bike. It's locked up just next to the post-room. That'll be the quickest way.'

Her other palm then appeared, revealing a set of keys to a bicycle lock. Hungry to prove myself a willing new employee, I grabbed them along with the batteries and hurried off.

Watching that cute show *Call the Midwife* on TV the other night, I was treated to umpteen scenes of the female stars cycling gracefully around the back streets of fifties London. Poised and pretty, they don't seem to have a care in the world (despite supposedly being in a rush to deliver the babies of hard-up, slum-dwelling Cockneys). This younger version of me, on the other hand, quickly found herself caught in the middle of a stream of cars, all apparently being driven by countless Jeremy Clarksons in a hurry to get home, with only the vaguest idea of how to get to the court house from our offices. Horns papped as I wobbled nervously into the middle of the road; cab drivers hollered as I dithered aimlessly at junctions and tried to remember the right way to go.

I can only imagine what my parents, already worried about my emigration to 'The Big Smoke', would have said if they'd known I was fumbling around W1 on the back of a two-wheeler (sorry Mum!). That said, my boss's bike was a ridiculously chic and hi-tech affair – one of those lightweight mountain bikes that probably cost as much as I was earning in a month. Should I fall off, I was less worried about my own injuries, more about chipping the paintwork on this work of art.

I had only two resources to guide me: an A to Z that I'd scanned briefly back in the office but which I had unhelpfully placed in my bag, and memories of childhood games of Monopoly. The Strand – that was one of the 'red' areas, near to Trafalgar Square, right? I felt for the batteries in my pocket before hooking an uncertain left and praying for guidance. I just needed to get the double AAs to Sophie and everything would be okay. I might even be deemed efficient enough to be given a real story to work on. And I would still be able to write, even with a leg squashed by an impatient London bus driver.

Over the years, I've got to know the bustling streets of sprawling Central London extremely well. I've had to. Showbiz events aren't confined to one place, despite Leicester Square being the most famous location for premieres. Swanky hotels from Mayfair to Embankment, Piccadilly to Covent Garden, fight with each other to host showbiz bashes, knowing that having a major record company or film studio as a regular customer would earn them thousands. I've been to some venues so many times, the concierge welcomes me like an old friend (although, I sometimes wonder if he realises I'm actually a journalist, not some hooker on a call-out). Now, I favour two feet over any other method of transport, what with buses being at the whim of traffic just like everyone else and the hassle of the London Underground hardly being worth it if the venues are central, and I can just as easily walk. I've also found that pacing the streets every week keeps you in shape almost as much as an intense session of Zumba down at the local sports centre would – and without the annoying instructor. On the days that I do have to take a cab I'm as familiar with the shortcuts and alternative routes as the drivers that take me. (My accountant may baulk at these taxi expenses every year, but has he ever tried to maintain a poker-straight blow-dry while walking in the pouring rain from Park Lane to Soho? I don't think so.)

One thing is for sure – I certainly wouldn't cycle any more. But, back then, on my mission, I was only just learning about the city's traffic chaos. Thankfully, after about 20 or so hellish minutes, I finally reached the court and handed over the batteries to a ridiculously thankful Sophie. I hung around for a few minutes, and watched as the musician who'd been in the dock that day came out on to the steps of the building to read out a statement. He'd been involved in a messy court case with former band mates, all of them arguing over royalties. Now he'd won, he looked relieved that it was all over. I knew how he felt.

Sophie was standing in among the throng of microphones and television cameras, holding out her dictaphone to record every word and even throwing in a few questions to the beaming pop star. Forgetful she may have been, but she was doing what I dreamt of doing.

Still, I had hope that one day soon I'd be given a chance. I'd already learnt several important lessons, after all:

1. Always be prepared and carry a spare packet of batteries.

2. Memorise the London street map like your life depends on it.

   Oh, and

3. Never cycle down Oxford Street at five o'clock in the evening.

   I wheeled the bike all the way back to the office.

Festivals

A few weeks after joining the magazine, having made a considerable amount of coffee and run endless errands, I finally got to do what I had been hired to do in the first place: report from some of that summer's music festivals. With a camera and notebook in hand, I set out to get a snapshot of the fashions and fads going on in remote fields that season, unaware that I was about to make a huge discovery about my career choice.

There are more festivals now than ever. Some are legendary, like Glastonbury and Reading; others are out of the way in small towns and normally feature a seventies dad rocker as a headline act. Every summer we have ample opportunities to pop on our jean shorts and cowboy hats, neck pints of warm cider and chill out in sunny fields for a weekend listening to bands we've never heard of. Sounds blissful, right?

Everyone knows that Glastonbury is amazing. Thousands of revellers gathered in a historic setting, all united by a shared love of music and partying. A loved-up crowd singing along to soaring anthems on a balmy midsummer night is a magical experience – at least, this is certainly what I had been told at school by my more adventurous mates, those girls whose parents weren't quite as panicky as my own and who seemingly lived a much more exciting life than mine by being allowed to travel miles to gigs. When I first got the job at the magazine, knowing that I was heading for the festivals, I couldn't wait to make up for lost time.

But this, it turned out, is not how it works for a showbiz reporter. It's hard enough as a regular ticket holder to plough through the mud and crowds to get from the dance tent on one edge of the camp to the main stage at the other in time for the headline act. As a showbiz journalist, with recording equipment and a deadline, you can multiply that difficulty by ten.

When you work in an industry that is – for most people – a leisure pursuit, you learn something very quickly: what was once your hobby is now your bread and butter. What you once did to chill out is now your job. That's not to say I don't still enjoy listening to music, watching the TV or going to the cinema as a pastime; it is, however, difficult to switch off completely. Maybe I've met the actor up there on the cinema screen and, since they gave me really boring answers to my questions, I'm finding it difficult to imagine them as a charismatic action hero (I'm talking about you, Nic Cage). Or perhaps the love song that I'm listening to, all heartfelt and emotional, is hard to swallow since its singer sadly seemed little more than a hard-nosed businesswoman when I met her (and that's you, Christina Aguilera).

It was during my outings to festivals that summer that I had my first taste of this. I was in work-mode, while seemingly everyone around me was soaking up the sun and smoking weed. I spent more time worrying about whether I'd get the interviews I needed than I did actually kicking back and enjoying the gigs.

The schedule of the festival season soon became engrained in my brain – and it still is. In recent years, the Isle of Wight festival, reborn after its legendary status in the 1970s, has been kicking things off in mid-June, but it's still Glastonbury a week or so later that really marks the start of a long summer in wellington boots. Then there's the riotous T in the Park in Kinross-shire, the arty Latitude in a Suffolk forest, the highly commercial V in both Chelmsford and south Staffordshire, the ear-splitting Reading and Leeds festivals, that take place over the same August Bank Holiday weekend as the rave-tastic Creamfields, and then it's all wrapped up at the quirky, boutique Bestival, which takes place back on the Isle of Wight where things all began ten weeks earlier. Not to mention a huge number of smaller festivals around the country and a plethora of branded events in virtually every park in London.

Despite the fact that it's never quite the same when you're attending them 'on the job', some of my experiences at these events were nothing short of incredible; bands always seem to try that bit harder at festivals – with such a variety of people in the crowd, they need to.

But there's one particular experience, a few years into my career, which will stay with me for ever. It was 2002; Rod Stewart was headlining Glastonbury on the Sunday and I'd spent most of the day on the phone trying to arrange an interview. Each time the answer from a record-company minion was the same: 'Maybe. Ask me later and I'll tell you where we are with things.' I'd walked from stage to stage trying to track down Rod's PR team, but to no avail. After a bit more searching and several more unsuccessful phone calls, the sun began to set over the Pilton hills.

With Rod presumably warming up for his set by gargling broken glass, the chances of meeting with my mum's favourite were frankly looking slim. I'd rung up a huge mobile bill and stressed myself out for nothing. With a heavy heart – and a resolution to erase 'Maggie May' from my iPod – I hung up my microphone for the day and headed over to the legendary Healing Fields, which were seemingly at least a mile away from the razzmatazz of the main stage. Determined to forget about work, I sat back with a 'special' chocolate brownie purchased from a stall nearby run by someone who frankly looked like a witch (albeit a nice witch), and basked in the final glow of the sun. Seemingly from nowhere, a girl about my age came up to me and offered to tattoo my hand with henna (feeling spontaneous, I accepted, obviously). A few feet in front of us, a group of women, all dressed in long white flowing robes, gathered in a circle and started to sing some sort of ancient madrigal about flowers and honey. As the luscious chocolate started working its magic, this song began to sound like The Greatest Thing I'd Ever Heard. Quite suddenly – and for the first time – I felt what the real Glastonbury was all about. Far away from the feisty crowds and the fast food and Rod Stewart and – crucially – reporting, I was finally relaxing into the true, love-filled, ancient spirit of the festival.

Back in London the next day the tattoo looked awful, of course, and my boss was highly annoyed that I had no interview with Rod for her to run. But that one moment away from the madness, away from the pressure, away from the aching legs and missed deadlines of being a showbiz journalist at a festival, was definitely worth it.

Some other favourite festival moments? Coldplay's first Glastonbury turn in 1999, when they were still just four nerdy university students who loved indie music, was a fabulous statement of intent. Jay-Z's Glastonbury headlining nine years later was a much-needed injection of American swagger into the West Country cow fields. And while I might not have been old enough to see the legendary turn by Nirvana at Reading in 1992, every time I've seen former member Dave Grohl headline a festival with the Foo Fighters it's been pure energy, passion and sweat. (Dave gives great interview.)

Of course, there are always musos who've been to a lot more festivals than I have, and each will relish describing to me – *a mere reporter* – a favourite that was supposedly 'the greatest gig ever' ('What?! You didn't see Amy Winehouse perform with a bunch of Indonesian nose flautists on the Save the Rainforest stage at 3 a.m. on Sunday morning back in 2007? And you call yourself a music fan?!'). Expert I may not be, but I still appreciate a good quality gig. I'm sure many of the bearded boys at Glastonbury were none too pleased when Beyoncé brought some pop bling to the farm in 2011 but personally, I couldn't get enough, though. Showbiz for me has always had talent and glamour going hand-in-hand.

Maybe that's another reason why *working* the festivals wasn't exactly a career highlight: wading through a muddy field at midnight when you haven't washed for 48 hours, you haven't eaten anything except a dodgy burger from a food van *and* you've got a deadline looming, can never be described as glamorous. The backstage press area where reporters lurk might boast proper toilets (I certainly don't care about the 'festival' experience when it comes to sanitation – I will defend my right to a toilet that actually flushes), but even home comforts can't get you an interview with Rod Stewart any more easily.

Premieres

Working premieres as a journalist can be fun simply because of the buzz. You can almost taste the expectation in the air, as you stand behind the rope, all your colleagues squashed up against each other (it helps to get on with other showbiz journos for precisely this reason), each of you excitedly uncertain as to what the next couple of hours will hold. In London there's a premiere roughly every week. The majority don't get the kind of blanket national press coverage that publicists dream of. But when they work, they *really* work, for both the film companies and the attendees. Liz Hurley turning up to the premiere of *Four Weddings and a Funeral* in a dress held together by safety pins made her name. Borat arriving at his premiere in a cart pulled by Kazakhstani peasant women guaranteed Sacha Baron Cohen a million column inches. And, while Julia Roberts forgetting to shave under her arms for the premiere of *Notting Hill* might not have been a planned publicity stunt, it got that movie more attention than the PR company could have dreamt of. Somewhere, some film producer is still counting his money and silently thanking a dippy LA maid for forgetting to pack Julia's razor. So, while many premieres come and go uneventfully, some change the face of showbiz. Who will turn up? What will they be wearing? Will the star of the movie stop and talk or not? With a well-known TV presenter usually hosting the night's events from a stage in Leicester Square and whipping the audience into a frenzy with promises of imminent arrivals, it's impossible not to feed off the energy of the night. Fans scream. Paparazzi flashes light up the night. Familiar reporters line the carpet with their cameramen, all hoping to get the best interview of the night. The red carpet has a magical pull. But as a journalist, there's also a downside; once the curtains go up, we have to go straight back to work. When the final celebrity has arrived, the final flashbulb has popped, the final interview wound up, it's back to the office we go to write up the night's events. The guests? Oh, they're in the cinema having a great time watching the film and thinking about how many free drinks and nibbles they can neck at the party afterwards. But me, I'm quickly shoved back into the real world; working late with only my computer screen and mug of cold tea for company, and listening back to the endless soundbites, trying to sniff out a sexy story from it all. As a showbiz reporter you get close to an extremely opulent and glamorous world – but never quite close enough. Which is why, when my first proper invite to a premiere arrived, I went a bit over the top . . .

I couldn't believe it. I had been working as a journalist for just over a year, and was well versed in the art of standing behind barriers on red carpets, waiting in the freezing cold for Celebrity X to turn up and possibly say a few words into my microphone. But now I finally had in my hands what I'd always dreamt of: a *proper* invite to a premiere. I looked at it again; even the gold lettering embossed on the thick cardboard was enough to get the butterflies in my stomach flapping like crazy. In just seven days I wouldn't be like all my colleagues, crammed into what's charmingly called the 'press pen' for hours. Oh no. I would be leaving my recording gear happily at home. My time as a voyeur would be over. I would be on the *other* side, glamorously swishing up the red carpet and mingling with the VIPs: a proper guest at a film premiere and party.

I had to start preparing. The bank of snappers gathered on their ladders might want to take my picture as I arrived; I had to look my best. I studiously practised posing in front of my bedroom mirror before I went to bed each night, drifting off to sleep with the imagined sound of a hundred camera shutters chiming melodically in my head.

Why was I invited? Errrr . . . That never really crossed my mind, to be honest. I'd had a couple of articles published in the magazine by this point, and I must have thought that I was making a name for myself. This was most likely a reward from a thoughtful film company for a complimentary story. In truth, the whole thing had made me a little ditzy. I wasn't used to special treatment. Suddenly, uncharacteristically, all I cared about was being thought of as 'someone' for the night – the mysterious girl on the red carpet that gets the crowds whispering . . .

'Who is she?'

'I've no idea. But if she's got an invite, she *must* be famous.'

'True. Over here strange lady! Over here! Sign my autograph book and let me have a photo taken with you!'

Vacuous, I know. But what can I say? I've never been fame-hungry, but I have always been fascinated by unlikely celebrities; people like Chantelle Houghton, the girl-next-door that posed as a star and ended up winning *Celebrity Big Brother*. During my short time as a showbiz reporter, I'd already come to realise that sometimes the main difference between 'the stars' and 'us' is attitude. The stars *believe* that they're worthy of fame, and as a result, it comes their way. It's all about conviction. I'd had very little opportunity to actually put this theory into practice, until now, with a red carpet to walk, where I could try it out.

*   *   *

The days before the big night seemed to last a lifetime. I even had to work another premiere in the run-up, and enviously watched the guests saunter up the red carpet without a care in the world. Very soon, I reassured myself, that would be me. I'd bought a new outfit for the occasion, something that was high street, but could never be described as 'just another dress'. With a low-cut neckline and swishing fishtail, I was out to make a statement. The day before, I humiliated myself by putting on paper knickers and allowing a stranger to spray me mahogany, to give me that LA radiance. Debuting the whole ensemble in front of my housemate Erica that night – who as my 'date' was also primping and preening like a *TOWIE* girl – I couldn't help but think back to the disparaging comments I'd had about my showbiz obsession back at college. Of course, interest rates and global warming are much more urgent topics of discussion than the latest blockbuster in the grand scheme of things, but nothing could compare to this for pure excitement. Showbiz *should* be exciting. Empty it may occasionally be, but is there really anything wrong with simple fun? Back at university, Erica and I had bonded over a mutual love of Ewan McGregor nude scenes and perfecting the moves to 'The Macarena', so I knew she'd be my perfect companion. The last person you want next to you at a premiere is someone who takes it all seriously.

Leicester Square seemed extra packed that night; clambering through the crowds to the start of the carpet proved especially difficult in four-inch heels, one of which I'd already managed to get unceremoniously stuck in the groove of a London Underground escalator. I was starting to feel a little sweaty from the exertion, and began to dream about the kind of chauffeur-driven limo that transports most celebs to premieres. I just had to hope I could pass off my hot flush as 'glow'.

Eventually we reached the security men who were guarding the sacred carpet from the great unwashed and, after flashing my tickets at them with a degree of smugness that even I was surprised by, we were let on to the crimson runway. It stretched ahead of us for about 100 metres, stopping just short of the cinema doors – but now was not the time to pull a Usain Bolt, I would be taking this slowly, savouring every second. On our left were fans and autograph hunters, many of whom would have been camped out since this morning in order to get a good position. On our right, the journalists, familiar faces largely, but they looked different from this angle, as if they were more bored than excited. But I didn't want to be reminded of my day job. I took a deep breath, blocked them out and began my journey.

And then came the deafening sound of . . . silence. As we strutted up the carpet, the colour drained even from my fake-tanned skin as I found myself being firmly put into place. No one shouted my name. No one took a photo. And, of course, from my colleagues in the press pen, there was not one request for an interview. All I saw on their faces was an expression that said 'Who does she think she is?'

I soon started to quicken my pace, desperate to get the whole experience over with quickly. I'd hoped to feel, just for a moment, like a part of the celeb world; in the end, I'd never felt further away from it. While a red carpet might feel like home for the famous, the screams of fans serving as a validation of their work, for someone unknown like me it is the loneliest place in the world.

Eventually inside, I had another humiliation to suffer. I bumped into a girl from a rival magazine, like me she was there as a guest, and was chatting to a group of people I knew from a local radio station. They'd been sent a whole bunch of invites too. Still dressed in their work clothes, they looked me up and down, smiled sympathetically at all the effort I'd gone to, then carried on their conversation. A journalist trying to be glam was obviously 'so not cool'.

Since that night, I've learnt an important lesson about premieres: eventually *everyone* gets invited. Of course, film companies send out wads of tickets – they want the event to look busy and buzzing. It wouldn't do to have empty seats at a premiere; after all, they don't want their star to look out from the stage as they introduce the movie only to be greeted by the sight of a half-full auditorium. So us 'regular' people in the media get invited. We're needed only for our bulk.

Erica gave my hand a reassuring squeeze as we walked down the aisle. We took our seats – just regular chairs at the back of a cinema I'd sat in many times before. The sheen was rapidly vanishing from the evening. More people, all of whom looked as if they'd come straight from the office, took the seats around us. The only 'celebrities' visible in the vicinity were a dance duo who'd found minor fame on a TV talent show a couple of years earlier. While the ticket may have said that we must be seated by 6.45 p.m. sharp, at 7.20 p.m. we were still no nearer to watching the film. We sat there waiting, uncertain what to say, munching loudly on the free packets of Maltesers that had been placed on our seats. I started to feel nostalgic for the cosiness of my office, with my dazzling computer screen and my trusty cuppa. Finally, after 45 minutes, the producer and stars of the film appeared on the stage to introduce the movie. But, as the lights went down, I saw them slip out of the fire exit with their entourages, heading off into the night to do something far more sexy and exclusive than watching their movie with a bunch of nobodies. I slipped off my high heels and curled up into the seat – as much as I could curl up in that bloody dress, anyway – wishing I could just go home.

Thankfully, I wasn't allowed to. The film, which to add insult to injury, was terrible, wrapped up and Erica virtually dragged me up to the waiting buses that were shipping us all out to a party venue down by the Thames. I knew that I was about to get a talking to.

'Holly Forrest, you listen to me. You might not be a superstar and the movie that you took me to might have sucked big time, but that's no reason for our night to end on a downer, okay? Let's get on this bus, let's sit on the back seat like naughty schoolgirls, then let's go to the party and drink too much and dance like idiots. Are you with me or are you with me?'

I swear Erica could have been a sergeant major in another life.

So that's exactly what we did. Until four in the morning, if you really want to know. And the best thing about all of it? Almost every celebrity we saw there looked miserable, unable to really let their hair down because they know it's never good to be photographed looking worse for wear. But us? We could do whatever we wanted and no one would care – two deliriously drunk, happily carefree nobodies.

Home life

In the same way that I only really understood a lot of *Absolutely Fabulous* after I'd started mingling with similarly hilarious PR women, I only really 'got' a lot of romantic comedy films once I'd started to analyse my own life as a media girl. On inspection, my day-to-day existence looked a lot like the plot of a Katherine Heigl movie – without the benefit of actually looking like her. It's no surprise that so many 'chick flicks' have their lead characters work in journalism (*The Devil Wears Prada*, *How to Lose a Guy in 10 Days* and *Confessions of a Shopaholic* to name but a few). It's a world rammed with confused women – women who, on the one hand, are desperate to prove themselves in a career by working every hour that God sends, but on the other wanting to lead a normal life: spend time with friends, have a relationship, maybe even a family. Of course, it is possible to do a bit of both. The fact that it's not exactly easy, however, is the kind of dramatic conundrum that every rom-com screenwriter in Hollywood wets themselves with excitement about.

Take my friendship group as a case in point.

It's a Sunday afternoon and I'm cosying up by the fire in my North London local with my friends, relaxing after a hard week (the previous Wednesday had witnessed the BRIT Awards – always exhausting) and enjoying a massive roast dinner. My housemate Erica is one of my oldest cronies, she's the kind of girl I can talk to about anything. She works in the media too, though less on the journalistic side and more in marketing. At work she's a ball-busting career woman who rules the roost. I've been to meet her at the office on a couple of occasions and seen her in action; her minions flock around her like an entourage around J-Lo. But when she's at home at night in our flat, laid out on the sofa with only a slanket and a Kate Hudson box-set to keep her company, she turns into Bridget Jones. I know that she could morph into a lover, girlfriend, even wife, very easily, the transformation just one online date away. For the moment, though, she seems happy enough being the classic chick flick singleton for whom work is her only significant other.

Then there's Ali, a fellow showbiz writer. She never stops either. Shops, bars, even doctors' surgeries all have their closing times. Ali, however, doesn't follow such specific hours. Her worklife is always ongoing, a 24-hour rollercoaster. It's exactly that which led to her break-up from a boy she'd been with for four years. He just couldn't stand the pace. Since the entertainment capital of the world, Los Angeles, is eight hours behind London time, there's simply no other way to cover a lot of breaking news than to pull an all-nighter. Four years of sharing your bed with his girlfriend's iPad was just all too much for him.

Then there's me. I won't go into detail as to what I was doing when I got the call, late one Thursday night in June 2009, that Michael Jackson was dead, but let's just say that jumping out of bed, throwing on some clothes and running out of the door swearing loudly isn't exactly conducive to passion. Especially when you can't even remember whose flat you're in. Not my classiest moment, but if I'm called in to do a shift, I'm called in to do a shift. As I sat forlornly in the back of the cab that Thursday night, trying to smooth my barnet into something that didn't look so obviously like 'sex hair', I could already imagine Drew Barrymore signing on for my biopic.

The media is littered with examples of what happens when work takes over. Stunning women, ladies who surely would be deemed 'a catch' by a multitude of men, are leading single lives well into their forties – not through choice, but through lifestyle. Sometimes, though, my colleagues just can't meet a guy because they simply don't have the time or the opportunity. Certainly, there are plenty of careers where the hours are long and erratic, but in the media – especially in showbiz – there's one extra challenge for women: you're on-call 24/7, in a work environment packed with more gay men than a Girls Aloud gig . . . Hell, even Katie Price would struggle to date with those odds.

Indeed, only my friend Danny has a serious relationship he can boast about, although not with another media-bod. Danny's partner has learnt to deal with Danny's career by simply not getting involved. His own career – a job in the City that Danny understands about as much as I do nuclear physics – is so far removed from Danny's job in radio that they keep things fresh by blissful ignorance. Both know their lives require them to do certain things the other would never comprehend, and they just accept that. For some people, your partner not showing an interest in your professional life might sound odd but after several years of trial and error, believe me when I say Danny's shown us all how it's done. His home life isn't constant chats about music or finance. It's about other stuff that has no link to work. That's got to be the healthiest way to keep alive a relationship two people so want to last.

Sadly, others find themselves on different paths. My friend Olivia was an events girl through and through, always seemingly at the end of her tether as she put together another showbiz bash or fended off another set of freeloaders looking for tickets to her latest party. She lived and breathed the job, albeit through a liver and lungs battered by regular intakes of gin and tobacco. Olivia would go home in the wee small hours, back to a flat with just QVC and a microwave meal to look forward to, despite having been working with glamorous stars and their publicists all day. That kind of contrast is one that seems even more painful when you reach middle age, as Olivia had. I think it's this contrast that led to her breakdown. Burnt out and bored with being too sick to work, Olivia pretty soon felt that she had nothing to fight for any more. Within a few months it was all over. Her memorial service was a gathering of colleagues who not only missed their old friend, but were silently praying they didn't end up like her. Sadly life doesn't have the happy endings of a rom-com.

So when I find myself working late, slaving over a story about weight loss or a feature on fashion, I constantly give myself reality checks. Showbiz is a big industry and one that fascinates millions – but for most of the time, it's just a bit of fun. Stressing over something that isn't the end of the world is pointless. If you do, it could be the end of yours.

Freelance

I worked for the magazine that first hired me for three years before I decided to spread my wings and go freelance. Since that day, I've worked for anyone who wants me. When my friends joke about me being 'a media tart' it's only really their cheeky choice of words that I can argue with. As a freelance showbiz journalist you'll do pretty much whatever is asked of you, as long as you're going to get paid for it. We dream of the easy, one-off, big money job – like Julia Roberts in *Pretty Woman* getting paid by Richard Gere to swan around Beverly Hills – but, ultimately, we're more streetwalker than high-class escort.

Okay, I think I'll stop the hooker analogy there.

I chose this life so I can't complain. After a few years as 'a staffer' I'd met enough people in the industry to realise that I could make things more interesting by being my own boss. With the amount of time we spend talking to other journalists while we're waiting around for stars to turn up at various events, it's easy to keep up to speed on what's happening employment-wise. I knew there was work out there, and my editor at the mag had promised to keep me on as a contributor. Plus, I'd already been offered work at another gossip mag. Working for two rival publications, however, isn't exactly encouraged, so I created some pseudonyms which I'd use to cover my back (no, I can't tell you what they are!) as so many freelancers do. Overall I couldn't wait to go solo.

A typical day? It's a lot less settled than it was when I was a staff writer. After getting up and scouring my favourite news sites – TMZ, MailOnline, Digital Spy – I'll either get dressed and head out for an interview or meeting, or I'll stay in my PJs and get writing. Resisting the charms of daytime TV is the real challenge. That said, on days when there's not so much going on, though, it's important to have a rest and spend time with family and friends. After all, you can't rely on weekends to be free. Recently I've being doing some shifts at an agency that requires me to work through the night – it's seriously tough. But knowing it's only temporary makes it all a lot more bearable.

News agencies are a hugely important part of journalism, yet most people don't even realise they exist. The fact is, so many things are happening in the world at any one time, no broadcaster or publication could possibly have enough reporters to cover them all. Instead, they subscribe to an agency service and use their material to fill in the gaps, material created by freelance journalists, like me. If an editor or producer has a space to fill in their newspaper or a 30-second hole in their radio news bulletin, a quick look at what the news agencies have sent over and their problems are often solved.

So it was that I came to have some of my interviews with celebrities used on TV, albeit with all signs of me totally erased. That's the thing with working for an agency. You're totally anonymous – a journalist with a one-size-fits-all style designed to appeal to any outlet that might want to use it. I actually liked the invisibility of, though. By the time I went freelance, my feelings about not wanting fame were solidified; I'd spent enough time around those who had it, to understand the restrictions it imposed on their lives. By now the last thing I wanted was to be one of those famous showbiz writers who splash pictures of themselves with celebrity 'friends' all over their articles. Working in the shadows, as I'd become accustomed to doing, you find that you still have a fair amount of influence, but none of the hassle. Sometimes becoming well known can be a career ruiner for a reporter. As soon as fame happens, interviewees become wary and put on more of a performance. Things get clouded.

Working as an anonymous writer for an agency also gives you a surprising amount of freedom. Now, at an interview, I can ask one type of question for one outlet and another type for a different outlet, knowing that I'll get paid for each one. These days I may find myself at a lot of the same events that I attended as a 'staffer', but I now have multiple remits and several bosses to please – a great way to keep me on my toes and help me avoid getting complacent. When I was a staff member at the mag, I have to admit, I tended to sleepwalk through some of the stories. I knew I'd be coming back to work the next day, so where was the challenge? As a freelancer, though, you're only ever as good as your latest story. Without contracts or written agreements, you can be unemployed in the blink of an eye. Intimidating it may be, but it also makes me try harder.

For a bit of extra pocket money, I also supply nuggets of gossip and information to showbiz sites. You might be surprised by how many reporters who are fully employed at magazines and TV stations also do this on the quiet. I'd illicitly done it myself a couple of times during my early career, but as someone always afraid of small print in contracts, I'd been wary of going overboard and ending up in trouble with my boss. Now I'm a freelancer, however, I can supply titbits to whomever I want. All journalists have their sources but many are also sources themselves. Knowing that a bit of information can put food on your table certainly keeps your senses keen.

The last few years haven't been easy, though. As the financial world continues to hover on the edge of a meltdown that I really don't understand, some work has dried up simply because companies can't afford to pay any more; getting a staff member who is already on a fixed salary to do some extra work costs nothing. Paying me, on the other hand, is a luxury that some outlets feel they can do without.

Despite the dangers involved with being self-employed, I love it. It only makes the buzz of getting a story even more exciting, more of a challenge. My accountant may wish that I'd never strayed away from the organised world of a staff job and a salary, especially when he looks at the state of my book-keeping, but I wouldn't change it for the world.

Bodyguards

Waiting around for celebrities might be part and parcel of my job, but no one has it as bad as bodyguards. A celebrity bodyguard needs to have the patience of a saint. Security men are meant to be on hand at all times to protect megastar X from any unwanted hassle or attention, but at the same time they have to be steadfast and invisible. In other words, they have a huge responsibility with none of the rewards. I encounter these boys all the time in my line of work – silent man-mountains who stand outside hotel-room doors or hover a few steps back on red carpets. Whatever is thrown their way, they display no emotion. As the owner of probably the worst poker face in the business, I never cease to be impressed by bodyguards.

Admittedly, even in all my years in the business, I've never actually seen a bodyguard have to do anything vaguely approaching combat. There has been the occasional moment where a bodyguard has had to spread their arms out wide to hold back the paparazzi or a bunch of hormonal teenage fans, but in all honesty, it seems that most of their time is just spent standing around, looking 'hard'. And, unless bodyguards have some kind of zen-like meditative strengths, they must be bored out of their minds. It certainly doesn't seem as exciting as Kevin Costner and Whitney Houston made it out to be.

Having security in one's employ appears to have become less about safety and more about status for celebrities. Katy Perry or Rihanna having a bodyguard is one thing, but I've seen random, mid-level male actors with them too – having a bodyguard as a mark of importance instead of for protection. There's a story that this is exactly what rock legend David Bowie did when he first went to America in the early seventies; Bowie supposedly hired an entourage of brutes to make him look like a superstar in a country where he was virtually unknown. With Bowie's famous theatricality that kind of works – he taught Lady Gaga everything she knows – but a boring B-Lister in need of an ego boost is something else altogether.

It was one of these B-Listers who became the subject of the only story I've ever wheedled out of a bodyguard. This lone security man was on hire 24/7, and one day found himself accompanying his 'celebrity' client on an all-night drinking session around the booze dens of London without, of course, being able to touch a drop himself. He stood and watched in bar after bar, all the while maintaining the appearance that he was ready to pounce on any crazed fan that might throw themselves on this star, even though he knew that was highly unlikely to happen. I got talking to the big man before a junket the next morning while he stood in a hotel corridor and, while not exactly talkative (getting bodyguards to crack a smile is difficult enough, let alone persuading them to talk), he was so exhausted that his normal reticence was certainly less on show. His charge was in his hotel suite, he told me, pointing to the door behind him. In a bid to recover from his long night of partying this Hollywood-nearly man was getting a rejuvenating massage and plentiful room service. All my burly friend had to prepare himself with was a black coffee and a muffin, hardly fuel for another long day of standing outside a hotel room, looking tough. 'I spent all bloody night playing gooseberry,' he said, his stony face finally cracking under the strain. 'I just had to loiter in the background as he snogged the face off some girl he picked up. And the worst thing is, he wants to do it all again tonight.' I got the story of the young Lothario into a couple of papers the next day, but I couldn't feel guilty – it made a pretty boring actor sound like a real stud, so I was probably doing him a favour.

As for the bodyguard . . . I salute you. You might think that being paid to essentially do nothing sounds like the greatest job in the world, but as my beefy friend will tell you, even doing nothing is tough when all you want is your bed.

Sources

It's two in the morning and I'm in a cab heading north after a night out in Soho, drunkenly watching the pounds on the meter going up and up and up. I make the same mental note that I always make in this situation, a worryingly regular occurrence: next time, Holly, just get the last train home.

Thankfully, my friend Daisy is in full swing:

'He likes both – girls *and* boys. Quite handy really. He's got this image of being a ladies' man – y'know, sells his films on it and everything – and the fact is, that's true. You can't argue with it. It's just that he also secretly bats for the other team too. Once you know about it, I actually think it's pretty obvious. Have you *seen* how much he hangs out with his mum, ha ha *ha*?'

No combination of letters could accurately capture Daisy's laugh, a piercing Cockney cackle that's potently amplified when lubricated with two bottles of wine. Be glad that you're only reading this, and not listening to it. But Daisy's great fun, and an even better source.

As a showbiz reporter you need to have a network of contacts to rely on for stories. It's true that these days a lot of gossip magazines and websites just make things up and try to pass it off as a fact by writing 'a source says'. And that's fine if the celeb in question isn't fond of taking people to court, or if they're a reality star who, as a breed, are normally so desperate they'll take any publicity they can get. In fact, they probably planted the story in the first place. For most of us, though, we need a source to get the facts needed for an article.

One of the few benefits of my dull journalist training is that I'm rigorous about my sources as a result. If a contact leads me to definite proof of a story, then their friendship is entirely worth the endless pounds I've spent on drinks and food in the bar cultivating it. Daisy is one of those sources; though we've become so close it thankfully doesn't feel like a business arrangement.

Daisy is a stylist-to-the-stars and a fount of information. For many celebrities, their stylist is their best friend. Most celebs aren't inherently chic. Sorry, but it's true. While our daily routine might only boast things as humdrum as running for the tube and painting our nails on the bus, a star's would include sessions with trainers and visits from manicurists and designers to make them look flawless. And it's understandable; if my picture was going to be in every gossip mag and website going then I'd invest in looking close to perfect too. Since being preened and pampered is such a regular occurrence for celebrities, they're often at their most relaxed around their team of beautifiers. The result? It's the stylists who overhear stuff no journalist could ever dig up on their own, be it discussions with managers about schedules, catty comments about another star in the industry ... or something even sleazier.

I met Daisy behind the scenes at an awards show and we've been friends ever since. She knows the deal. Her revelations alone are unlikely to end up printed word-for-word online, but the nuggets she feeds me often morph into bigger stories. I think she rather likes the playground superiority of being able to say 'I know something you don't', and I know she likes the idea of being someway party to a world that isn't her own – the world of journalism. Most importantly, though – and this is crucial for a source – Daisy and I like having a few drinks and a gossip together.

She tells me a lot of stuff, of course, that I can do nothing with. If a star she's working with is secretly trying for a baby with her boyfriend then I'm not going to blow their cover. There's no scandal there; it's all too personal. If that boyfriend is actually a front, though, a cover for the relationship she's having with another woman, but is too desperate for mainstream stardom to admit it? Well, I'm not so keen on letting people get away with lying.

One night over a bottle of red Daisy told me about a recent client – a slightly square middle-aged thespian renowned for his earnest acting – who spent his half hour of being dressed for a photo shoot making lewd suggestions to her. When he'd had enough of her rebuffs, he telephoned a mate and was even more crude about the teenage starlet he was currently starring in a film with. Thanks to Daisy, I've been closely watching this chap ever since. If the tip-off is anything to go by, he'll have a sexual harassment case hanging over him within a year.

As well as a stylist, there are other 'insiders' it's always useful to be friends with. Such as:

The hotel concierge. Trying to find out if a star really is in town? London might be a city boasting thousands of hotels, but in reality the rich and famous only ever stay at a handful. And I'm not talking about Travelodges or Holiday Inns. Having someone on the ground in Mayfair's swankiest accommodations is always worthwhile, even if they often only answer my questions with a simple 'yes' or 'no'. It was a 'yes' that I heard down the line when I asked a concierge contact at a top hotel if a certain pop star was staying there. Not a story in itself, perhaps, but it certainly gave credence to the rumours we'd heard that his wife had kicked him out of the marital home. As a renowned drinker and party animal, that was going to be one big mini-bar bill.

The door whore. I will be eternally grateful to the guy who used to control the guest list at one particularly poncey club in Central London. It's not that the place was even my scene – the drinks were overpriced and the decor was more S&M dungeon than classy lounge – but through a few visits with friends, I'd got to know him reasonably well and one night it paid off. A famous pop star had been strenuously denying he was marrying his girlfriend that week, but it was rumoured they would both be partying with friends down in this basement hangout for an impromptu joint stag and hen do. As I trotted up to the door, my friend with his clipboard 'umm-ed' and 'aah-ed' and generally became a drama queen for a few minutes, but ultimately he let me downstairs. Yes, he knew why I wanted to go down there, but he also knew that a bit of publicity about his club being the venue for such a rock 'n' roll party wouldn't do him any harm either. After spotting the happy couple in a corner, I sent a text to a photographer friend to wait outside for a shot of them leaving then went about the business of noting everything the duo were drinking, eating and dancing to. Combined with the snap of them coming out of the club at 3 a.m., the piece I wrote prompted more than one person to comment on it being 'so detailed, it's like I was there'. I didn't have the heart to tell them it was because I was.

The clinic receptionist. When you work in a job where celebs take you into their confidence, it's understandably difficult not to get carried away. You become party to some pretty juicy gossip – gossip many would pay you for – and it's only human to succumb sometimes to temptation. That was certainly the case with one receptionist at a plastic surgery clinic who I had in my confidence. Camp as Christmas and eager to share his star spots, I always found out pretty quickly which megastar was having what done to their nose, eyes or forehead. When one of those 'have they or haven't they?' articles is mooted at a morning meeting, I have all the names immediately to hand. And while we are careful not to state anything as 'fact' in a feature, there is no uncertainty in my mind as to whether those names have had work done or not. Every single one, according to my loose-lipped receptionist, will have passed through his doors in the last year. And to think they all put their beauty down to just having 'good genes'.

The publicist. It's assumed that publicists have to follow some kind of moral code, meaning that all their work is officially set up and planned – sit-down interviews for a magazine or studio photo shoots with a top snapper, for example. If only life were that innocent. Getting your client into the press is now a shame-free exercise and publicists are more likely to be heavily suggesting stories and angles to showbiz journalists than waiting for a more traditional promo opportunity to come up. The old adage that 'no publicity is bad publicity' is truer than ever, and publicists will tip off the paparazzi with something as pointless as their client walking down the road in a particularly skimpy dress. I've lost count of the number of times I've been spun the yarn that the good-looking but frankly talentless Mr X is in talks to go over to Hollywood and make a movie, but with an ever-increasing number of spaces to fill in magazines and websites, sometimes that kind of story – however tenuous – is just what I need.

Ten past two in the morning and the cab is dropping me off at my flat. I hand Daisy 20 pounds to cover my share of the fare and remind myself once again to get the train next time.

'Bye darlin', ha ha ha!' Daisy shouts through the taxi window, apparently not caring about everyone trying to sleep. 'Let's do it again soon, yeah?'

'Definitely,' I reply, trying not to stumble up the kerb.

'And make sure you remind me – I must tell you about this singer I've been working with. Was the face of a charity campaign and claimed to be all "right on" about it, y'know. Actually she was getting paid a fortune for it. She couldn't give a shit about hungry Africans.'

My ears prick up, sensing a story.

'Dais, you're a star. Same time next week?'

Flirting

There was this one actor – a pretty boy who looked as if he spent more time than I did preening himself – who simply took my breath away when I met him. Wow was he beautiful. Puppy dog eyes, a Celtic accent, and bee-stung lips that looked even more kissable in real life than they did projected on to a 15-foot cinema screen – I was smitten. I suspect that he'd had one of those long, tedious days of promotion because, when I walked into the interview room I sensed immediately that he was up for some fun. 'Chemistry' is the kind of cheesy word used by dim WAGs talking about their latest footballer boyfriend, but there was definitely something scientific happening when he and I talked. Well, I say talked. We giggled. We flirted. Any talking we did was the kind of hilarious-at-the-time nonsense that's more suited to a drunken pub date than a professional interview. Still, I left 20 minutes later buzzing from all the pouting and eyelash batting that had just taken place – and that was just from him.

'How did it go?' my editor asked as I handed over the tape so that she could choose the best bits to send out to the radio stations we supplied to (I was working for a news agency at the time). 'Amazing,' I said, beaming. 'We got on *so* well. Have a listen. You'll really like it.' Fifteen minutes later, my editor is at my desk, her usually pasty complexion red with fury. 'The interview,' she began, 'is frankly unusable. It's just the noise of two people giggling. I don't doubt that you may have had a wonderful time together but no one wants to hear two kids' foreplay on the radio.' She slammed the tape back on my desk and strode off in a huff.

I know – it probably sounds wildly unprofessional to flirt in the work place, but this is showbiz. Let me explain.

It's no exaggeration to say that many of the guys who go into showbiz do it to 'get laid'. Ask any rock star, actor or presenter why they chose their line of work and, after a bit of embarrassed bluffing, you're bound to get the same answer: sex. Perhaps it's no surprise that so many famous creative men were complete geeks at school who couldn't get a girlfriend. The young Chris Martin, it's fair to say, was no obvious sex symbol in his youth. It is when these guys realise that belting out a rock tune or delivering a line can attract beautiful women that their career path becomes very clear. Hence Chris married Gwyneth. So if you're a Billy No Mates reading this, take my word for it – get on the stage or screen or start playing guitar and your virginity woes will be over.

But it goes even further. Once you're working in the entertainment world you quickly realise that there's *so* much time to kill. Film sets are the slowest moving places in the world; actors spend hours in their trailers waiting to be called. World tours, meanwhile, just mean endless hours on the road and in hotel rooms. What better way to while away the time than chatting up anything that moves?

My male friends have essentially no stories to recount of flirting with female stars. Seriously: zilch. I suppose one reason for this is that there just aren't as many male showbiz journalists out there, and of that already small number, a high proportion are gay. Even if Taylor Swift wanted to find a new squeeze while promoting her latest album, she'd struggle with the measly crop of boy journos on offer. But if Russell Brand wanted to do the same thing? He'd be inundated with women. Indeed, he'd be inundated with attractive women; many female showbiz journalists are wannabe TV presenters who know that to get ahead in the industry, you need to look polished and pretty. Line up 30 of us in front of a rock band on press day and it's only human nature as to what might happen.

After sending out a bunch of questioning emails to 14 of my closest female colleagues the other day, I got back the following responses:

1. Have you ever had a male celebrity flirt with you? Eleven said yes.

2. Has a male celebrity ever asked to hang out with you outside of work? Six said yes.

3. If yes, did you actually go? Three did.

4. Finally, have you ever actually slept with a male star that you've interviewed? Again, three.

I know the few straight male showbiz reporters there are will be reading those numbers with envy.

I've certainly experienced the libido of male stars on a few occasions. I can't pretend to be totally innocent either; knowing just how bored these guys get doing endless rounds of interviews, maybe I've put on an extra-short skirt or low-cut top that day to keep them interested. Get your interviewee's attention and who knows: maybe it's not just your neckline that's got a scoop? You see flirting can be fun *and* profitable.

For the most part, flirtation stays within the interview-room walls. But even then, there's a problem. Listen back to the interview later and you'll soon realise the sound of two people chatting each other up isn't that exciting for anyone but those two people. It's the old story of 'you had to be there'. I learnt that lesson the hard way: following 'flirtgate' with my doe-eyed actor, my editor stayed in a huff with me for the best part of a week.

So while I'll still wink at the latest showbiz beefcake without any shame, I now know my limit. Have a laugh, but don't make your audience feel like they're voyeurs to the early stages of lovemaking.

Next time I interviewed the pouty beauty he'd forgotten that we'd ever even met. He answered my questions with a bored demeanour and several glances at his watch. That's the thing about actors – so many mood swings they make PMT look like a walk in the park. My editor thought *that* interview was great, though.

Like many of my colleagues, I've actually been asked out by a cheeky star too . . . Well, sort of. The guy in question had been a big name in the nineties, but was now reduced to straight-to-DVD fodder. (I can't even remember the name of the dodgy low-budget action movie that he was in town plugging.) As a veteran of the promotional trail, he was probably more bored than most when it came to doing interviews, but I suspect that he also wanted to prove to himself that he still held some sway as a rebel-rousing heart-throb. Hence the email I got when I was back in the office after the interview. It was a note from his publicist – someone I'd met for the first time only a few hours earlier – asking if I would consider a drink that night with 'her client'. Yes, it was that impersonal. I had noticed a significant amount of silly flirting between us in the hotel interview room, but it was so over the top I'd assumed it was just a joke. Not wishing to be just another notch on a hotel bedpost, I said no this time. I couldn't feel bad for him.

He had at least another day of interviews to do and that meant a lot more female reporters he could get his publicist to ask out for him. A dirty dog he may have been but deep down he was obviously just a big chicken.

Johnny Depp

There's one question that almost everyone asks me when they find out what I do for a living: 'So, er . . . have you met anyone famous then?'

It's not exactly the most brilliant piece of questioning. It's my job to meet famous people, so of course the answer will always be yes. It's a bit like asking a hairdresser if they've ever cut a fringe. When that bit of banter is out of the way, however, the line of enquiry often goes in one direction:

'So, er . . . have you met *Johnny Depp*?'

Whoever I'm speaking to – from a giggly teenage girl to a thirty-something film buff – everyone wants to know about Johnny. At the mere mention of his name, eyes widen and broad grins appear. More than any other star I know of, he appeals to all ages and all genders. Maybe these people don't even go and see all of his films, certainly not the more eccentric ones Johnny has a taste for, but that doesn't seem to matter. It's *him* that they want to know about, his personality and his quirks. So for all the people who want to know, here's my take on the man behind Captain Jack. I can't claim to have got as close to him as Kate Moss or Vanessa Paradis – more's the pity – but we've met on a few occasions and, unsurprisingly, they're not moments I've forgotten about.

From those few times I've come to realise that Johnny is basically a pretty mixed-up fella – but in the best possible way. He's a man with many sides to him. As an actor, he's a chameleon who clearly relishes a chance to go a bit nuts, and a rebel with a funny hat and silly accent. As an interviewee, on the other hand, he's a kitten. I call him the 'well-mannered wild man'. It's a confusing but exciting mix.

I first met Johnny Depp way back, before the *Pirates of the Caribbean* franchise turned him into such a megastar that, frankly, he doesn't really need to do much press any more. Prior to setting his knee-high boots upon the deck of the *Black Pearl*, Johnny was just another cool actor; one that created fascinating characters and worked with interesting directors, maybe – but just another actor who had to do interviews like everyone else.

You could tell that he didn't necessarily enjoy the process. On our first meeting, which took place in a hotel room in New York, he walked into the room with the body language of a doddery old relative who ambles around wondering exactly where they are and what they're doing. When he finally seemed to switch on to what was going on, he sat down next to me, and politely but quietly said hello. I began the interview.

To say that when Johnny opened his mouth to reply to my questions he wasn't exactly Mr Extrovert is the understatement of the year, but I don't mean it as a criticism. Quite the opposite; in fact, it only made me like him more. As the chat went on he transitioned from the senile grandparent into a lost child, answering questions with a fragile air and a tender tone. I wanted to mother him. He was so polite and attentive it was as if he was from another, more dignified, era. Of course, with actors this talented you have to ask yourself if this was actually all an elaborate scam to make me like him more. Unfortunately, it's never easy to tell. But whether real or fake, it was working. His boyish gentility was a real vote winner.

This was certainly not what I had expected. Johnny Depp, it's fair to say, has experienced his fair share of wild times – rebellious years of partying and punching photographers. I had anticipated much more of a libertine, than the gentleman sat opposite me. But interviewing Kiefer Sutherland, another reformed hell-raiser, a few months later I noticed a trend. Like Johnny, former-playboy Kiefer was also quiet and courteous. I came to realise that these guys might have their riotous moments, but when they're on a break from revelry, they're just sweet, smart and old-fashioned. Their dangerous side isn't relentless and Neanderthal, like sexed-up teenagers on holiday in Kavos. I noticed something similar with Pete Doherty, an archetypal bohemian rocker and party-goer who also has the brains of a swot and the manners of an Enid Blyton character.

Once I'd got past Johnny Depp's soft-voiced and sensitive side, the darker side of him soon was clear to see too. It was right there in the way that he dressed. His guitar-playing fingers were covered in rings, many in the shape of skulls. His hair was long and lank, the iconic rock 'n' roll barnet. And on that exquisitely chiselled face stubble was messily growing into a goatee. Here was a guy who could have joined the line-up of Nirvana and nobody would have batted an eyelid.

And there, in a nutshell, is his appeal. Date a real rocker and you're likely to play second fiddle to his drinking, womanising and endless guitar solos. But with Johnny you get the looks of a music god, alongside the personality of a puppy. Not a bad combo, eh? He's the best of both worlds. No wonder every woman from here to Wonderland is in love with him.

A couple of years later, when a second opportunity to interview

Johnny came around, I was more prepared for these intoxicating ingredients. Little boy lost? Yep, I could handle it. Bohemian god? Ready for that too. This time, however, I also discovered yet another dimension: his sense of humour.

As cameos in TV sitcoms such as *The Vicar of Dibley* and *Life's Too Short* demonstrate, Johnny Depp's got a soft spot for British comedy, and I think that's part of the reason that we Brits have a soft spot for him. When it comes to making people laugh, he's much more Monty Python than *Two and a Half Men*. When I met Johnny second time around, it was obvious from his lack of energy that he'd had a long day of interviews. So, I changed tack and aimed squarely for the funny bone. I threw a bunch of absurd questions at him about crazy internet stories and wild rumours, and it worked, he seemed a lot more happy with this angle than answering the sensible, probing questions I'd opened with. Because alongside that wannabe rock star personality with the heart of a sensitive 10-year-old, Johnny also just wants to play the fool. The crazy, surreal and odd are what seem to get him through life, and in Hollywood there's plenty of that weirdness to feast on. After joking around for a few minutes, his vitality returned (although that could have been down to the goblet of red wine he was quaffing or the strange, black cigarette that he puffed on every few seconds). Johnny Depp – the *witty*, well-mannered wild man.

I was looking forward to seeing him again uncovering yet another aspect of his appeal, but something awful happened: megastardom. The *Pirates of the Caribbean* films turned Johnny from an edgy indie actor into a global superstar. Since then, getting to him has never been quite as easy. Once his family had come along, he became even more protective of his private life. And with a bank balance the size of a small country's, the need to flog his movies to every showbiz hack out there became less of a concern. When I read about his break-up from Vanessa Paradis, his long-term partner and the mother of his children, I felt saddened that even those who try to avoid the limelight can still fall prey to the long shadows it casts. I suppose when you're away from each other for so long it's almost impossible to keep a normal relationship – whether you're Jack Sparrow or Joe Bloggs.

But in answer to that question I'm now so familiar with, what's Johnny Depp like? Well, he seems to be one of the good guys. Yes he's sexy. Yes he's cool. And that mash-up of danger and innocence make him my favourite actor, not only to watch but also to talk to. I just wish he'd talk more often.

Junkets

There is no normal day 'at the office' for me. I'm out and about too much. While some people might not like that kind of existence, I love it. Before I was a freelancer, when I was working full-time at the magazine, our office block was so dreary I couldn't wait to get out. It was amazing that a publication so glossy and glam could come out of such a bland environment. I still drop in there sometimes and little has changed. Inside it's all open plan, and most people have tried their hardest to brighten things up a little, putting a plant here or a poster there, but it looks no less like David Brent's stomping ground. I'd much rather be spending my time in a chic Soho hotel and staring at interior-designed wall art than the gurgling water fountain that sat near my former desk. Thankfully, a lot of my time is taken up at junkets in exactly those kinds of hotels, so I frequently find myself surrounded by ridiculous luxury. Okay, it might remind me how little money I have, because I could never *actually* afford to stay at those kinds of places, but it's still infinitely preferable to standing around queuing for the photocopier.

Junkets – I know, silly name isn't it? Google it and you'll find that most entries describe an antiquated kind of dessert, a strange custardy mousse-type food that originates back from medieval times. Quite what that has to do with the modern usage – meaning an organised press day – I have no idea. Still, whenever I try to explain to a layperson what a junket is, there's an easy point of reference. Remember that bit in *Notting Hill* where Hugh Grant is so desperate to see Julia Roberts that he sneaks into her press interviews posing as a journalist from *Horse & Hound*? Well *that's* a junket.

In reality, junkets run on schedules so tight that no one could just rock up on the day and bluff their way in, especially not someone from a hunting magazine (even if they do look like Hugh Grant). Nevertheless, the film certainly captures the mood perfectly. In a word, they're awkward. You may be holed up in a posh London retreat (think The Dorchester or Claridges, never actually The Ritz, the hotel featured in *Notting Hill*), but there's still an overwhelming sense of sitting nervously in a surgery waiting room as you huddle up next to fellow reporters, sometimes for hours on end, twiddling your thumbs and dreaming of your name being called.

Although music and TV stars sometimes do junkets to promote new material, on the whole these are the preserve of the film industry. Watch breakfast television where the presenter is seen interviewing a famous actor in some dark little room with only a movie poster in the background for decoration, and you'll be witnessing the result of a junket. Why take an actor to a load of different radio and TV stations when reporters from those places could all just gather in one place and interview the actor one after another? If that sounds like a bit of an assembly line then that's because it is, albeit one in hotel rooms that cost £500 a night.

I certainly don't cover every junket – there's usually a couple in London every week – but whenever I do the experiences are much the same. In a job where you're constantly reacting to the latest news, rarely knowing what the day ahead will hold, junkets are reliably predictable. Here's how the average junket works: I go to the hotel and make my way to an assigned room half an hour or so before the first interview is scheduled. I then check in with one of the glossy PR girls who are running the show. The girl will more often than not tell me that 'Celebrity X is running a bit late I'm afraid.' I am well aware that 'a bit late' actually means around an hour late. I sigh. I then get shown to another room (that is basically a bedroom that's had the bed taken out). It is packed with my fellow showbiz reporters and I sit down and count down the minutes, stocking up on cups of that posh coffee that comes in little pods that you have to put in a machine. When I first started this job I had no idea how to use such a contraption. Now I've spent so much time in junket waiting rooms with them, that I could gracefully whip you up an espresso faster than a Formula 1 tyre change. While blindfolded.

After about four cups, three toilet visits and endless staring at my notes, a girl clad in black with a clipboard strides purposefully over to me, ushers me out of the waiting room and down the corridor into another, smaller room where there are more glossy PR girls with clipboards waiting for me. They in turn do some more ushering – PR girls are really very good at it – this time towards the famous person sat in a chair, who is waiting to be asked as many questions as I can fit into the four-minute interview slot. At last! If the film's a big one with nearly all the cast available for interview, then I can find myself not seeing daylight for the best part of a day as I traipse from one room to another, fuelled up on the pastries and beverages I sneak from the waiting room between interviews. If I get to meet a star I've always liked and if the interview goes well, then a junket can be a joy. If it goes badly, after all that loitering, then to be honest, they're a pain in the arse.

And it does often go badly. You see, junkets for the talent are a mind-numbing experience, a relentless trudge of interviews where umpteen shiny showbiz journos ask them the same questions over and over again (a film that captures this even better than *Notting Hill* is actually another Julia Roberts gem, *America's Sweethearts*. The problem for us journalists is that many stars are very bad at hiding their boredom. We often find ourselves waiting in that hospitality room from 9 a.m. to midday, only to finally be greeted by an actor or director who's frankly fed up with having to talk about the film. Actors may get paid millions per film, but that cash it's often said isn't actually for appearing in the movie. That's the fun bit. No, the paycheque is for taking part in the brain-frying publicity trail that takes place just before the film comes out.

So there I am, an A-Lister sat just a few feet in front of me. I'm tired, having waited for the past 90 minutes twiddling my thumbs. And the talent's bored, having been asked 'Why did you do this movie?' and 'What's it like working with . . .?' 37 times already that day.

There will be someone sat to my right holding a stopwatch to make sure I don't overrun my strictly allotted time (one junket they even placed a giant digital clock right in my eyeline, the numbers counting down like some kind of missile launch procedure). On my left there might be the star's personal publicist, tapping away on their smartphone but all the while monitoring my questions for anything vaguely controversial that they can shout at me for. This is clearly not the ideal set-up for a great interview, but somehow I'm expected to bond with my interviewee, to make it look as if we're both having fun and, most importantly, get some kind of scoop.

This does happen occasionally, though it rarely goes to plan. I once interviewed a Hollywood starlet who at the time was rumoured to be having a fling with her co-star, a musician who was having his first stab at acting. Both were at the junket but, of course, asking either of them about the rumours outright was a big 'no-no'. He'd been about as interesting as a council meeting in his interview with me, so I was relying on her to spill a few beans about him . . . er . . . spilling his beans. No such luck. As Miss Stopwatch started to wind me up with a frantic circling of her index finger, I had pretty much resigned myself to not getting anything decent out of the day. The actress was sweet but guarded – the worst kind of interviewee. Rubbish. I thanked everyone and headed out of the room, defeated. Until . . . who was this passing me in the doorway to the room? I recognised him from our very recent meeting. Surely it wasn't her co-star and possible squeeze sneaking in to have a quick catch-up? You bet it was.

'Hey baby!' he calls over to her. 'We still good for tonight?'

'Hell yeah. I cannot wait. I've missed you.'

The door closes behind me, but I'd heard all I needed. These two were way more than just friends, I was sure. 'I've missed you'? 'Baby'? I'd never even use that language with a boyfriend. As I left the hotel, I called up a friend from a mag with one of those 'Wicked Whisper' columns, full of rumours about A-Listers. She *loved* the story. The next day I get my first scoop in a national tabloid, with me referred to only as 'a source', of course.

A few weeks later the two stars were papped together in LA, hand-in-hand, officially a couple – but I'd got the story first. You see that's the thing about junkets: the interviews are frequently dull, clinical affairs, but what goes on between the interviews can be anything but. It's the person that a star becomes when the microphones and cameras go off that's *really* interesting. Without any hard proof, not everyone's going to believe you. But there's always someone willing to take a risk.

So the hours I'd spent waiting for those interviews hadn't been entirely wasted. I not only had regular interviews with the movie's stars for my main employer, I'd also sold a secret story to another: a freelancer's dream.

The Family

I hope by now I've started to give you an idea of what this job involves, but I should probably mention that 'showbiz journalist' actually covers lots of different breeds of reporter. A variety of sub-groups make up the whole profession. We're all part of the same family (which I overheard be disparagingly referred to as 'drongos' by a publicist that didn't realise I was in earshot), and we might cross paths every now and again, but that's where the similarities end. We're quite the species. National Geographic could make a whole TV series about us.

Type 1 – *The tabloid journo*
The most ruthless showbiz reporter of them all. These are the guys whose pages so many people flick to in the newspapers or online every day, to hungrily read the latest boy band scandal or to laugh at pictures of the latest party girl falling out of a nightclub and flashing her knickers. The tabloid journalist is very much the face of showbiz journalism – larger-than-life gossip hounds whose relentlessness is as impressive as it is sometimes morally dubious. In the press, being a showbiz editor can be a fast-track to an even bigger career in journalism. Take Piers Morgan. (No please, take him.) Yes, everyone's favourite smug chat-show host and talent-show judge

was formerly the merciless editor of *The Sun*'s showbiz column for five years. That's a pretty impressive transition. If you can make the grade as a daily entertainment hack then, it seems, you can do anything. Interestingly, after the laddish days of Piers and his peers, today's wave of tabloid journalists (led by internet sensation Perez Hilton) seem to be more mincy than macho. But that effusive exterior is often a great way to mask a cut-throat ambition. These guys are all a lot of fun to hang out with; just don't expect them to put down their BlackBerrys for the whole night.

Type 2 – the telly babe

Of course, some entertainment correspondents on hard-hitting television news shows are expertly trained and rigorously educated. However, when it comes to showbiz news, it's mainly covered by the fluffier side of programming, and those types of outlets know exactly what they want from their reporters: sexiness. Attend any showbiz event and it's obvious which girls and boys work in telly, they'll be groomed and glamorous, and when it comes to interviewing, they're mainly out to strike up repartee with the star rather than to display an acute sense of journalism. A lot of TV shows now employ interviewers who themselves are famous – recognisable from a reality show or a high-profile fling. Who needs a trained journalist asking questions when you've got a pretty face that's been in the gossip mags? As someone who occasionally has to write those very articles celebrating the latest WAG or talent-show wannabe, I sometimes wonder whether I'm just doing myself out of a job. When you've got bills to pay, though, you can't be too choosy.

There is a crucial difference between us showbiz journalists and the celebrities that sometimes do our work, though. For many of these TV hotties, their own fame is as important as the famous people they're interviewing. They're in it for their profile as much as in the interest of extracting insightful answers from an A-Lister.

True, I've had my moments where I've dreamt of being this kind of reporter – as have most of my colleagues, I'm sure. Ultimately, though, fame isn't for everyone. I like my privacy far too much to ever want to have my face exposed in the way these guys do, however expertly made-up and pouty their faces might be.

Type 3 – the radio reporter

'They've got a great face for radio' the old phrase goes – and it's often bang on. People who work on the radio simply don't need to make the effort their TV cousins do because, by and large, they're not going to be seen. For this type of reporter, it's all about 'content over style'. And I love them for that. Radio might just be the last corner of broadcasting where being able to communicate incisively is still deemed to be more important than how high your profile is. A lot of radio showbiz reporters work for agencies that supply snippets of entertainment news to stations around the world; their voices are familiar to millions but their looks and personality are happily hidden from the outside world. That posh BBC announcer who crops up all the time on Radio 4 (Kathy Clugston) might have a voice that's instantly recognisable, but I haven't got the faintest idea what she looks like. While radio might not always be the glossiest part of the media to work in, it's incredibly important.

Type 4 – the magazine writer

This is still my main territory and I'm rightly protective of it. It's true that the publications I work for are hardly *New Statesman* or *The Spectator*, but I'm at least allowed a bit more time to craft a piece than newspaper writers with daily deadlines to meet. Though the rise of our online news sites has meant that there's more pressure to come up with quick features to go online, generally speaking, we're not like those stressed hacks who'd sell their own dog to get a scoop into the paper the next day. I'm not out to stitch anyone up. I have dabbled in all of the other types of showbiz reporter that I've mentioned – one of the joys of being freelance – but I always come back to the magazine world when I can. The big guns of the print world still hold a lot of sway in the media and I get a kick being associated with some of the most famous names in publishing. Even better, unlike a lot of my colleagues who work directly in the spotlight and whose names are well known, my tiny bylines in magazines are great places to hide.

The movie of my life

Tonight is cocktail night and we're in Soho talking about work. Actually we're just gossiping about showbiz in the way that most people like to when they're having a drink, but when showbiz *is* your work, your job and your hobby merge into one. As usual, the chat about who we've met recently turns into our favourite game: 'Who would star in a movie of your life?' We've played it many times before, but with an ever-changing showbiz scene – as well as our ever-changing hairstyles – the actor who was spot-on last year might be totally unsuitable now. The first time I ever played it was an unforgettable (and regrettable) night of sambucas, where it was widely agreed that Mischa Barton, from the American TV drama *The OC*, should play me. Back then I couldn't have been happier. I *loved* that show; full of the hottest young stars, with the coolest music of the time on the soundtrack. Ten years later and Mischa's better known for her arrests, psychiatric confinement and range of handbags available on shopping channels. So, sorry Mischa, but I'm just not so keen any more. Even in my fantasy I want someone with box-office clout.

My friends are easy to cast. Posh Petra, a girl who works in 'events' (i.e. sends out party invitations) has just copied me and gone auburn. Suddenly she's a dead spit of Emily Blunt. Ali, my lovely-but-nuts pal that works at a rival mag, clearly has Kristen Wiig in a filthy comedy written all over her. Her life makes *Bridesmaids* look like *Last of the Summer Wine*. Then there's Danny. Every time we play this game he envisages his biopic as an intense, *Brokeback Mountain*-style drama, picturing himself dreamily as Jake Gyllenhaal. After much arguing he normally concedes and admits that he's actually much more like a slightly camper Jack Black.

'What about you, Holly? Who'd be you in your film?'

'Well, Holly's obvious,' chips in Danny, before I can even open my mouth. 'Kat from *EastEnders*!'

I punch his leg and wait for the raucous laughter to die down. With Mischa in the wilderness I know I have to go for someone more current. Since Jessica Chastain is not only an Oscar nominee but also looks like the kind of committed actress that wouldn't mind changing her looks a little for the role, I'm going to plump for her, and admittedly she'd also need to 'plump' a little to play me. I'd probably go the whole hog with casting legends Tommy Lee Jones as my dad and Meryl Streep as my mum. You might as well aim for the awards, right?

As for my love interest . . . that's where fantasy really takes over from reality. I'd have to cast a crush of mine since my childhood, a man whose star never seems to wane. Despite being better known as a TV presenter, he has acting credentials. So ladies and gentlemen, prepare yourselves for Jessica Chastain in *Confessions of a Showbiz Reporter*. Co-starring Declan Donnelly, aka Dec from Ant & Dec. Probably not coming soon to a theatre near you.

Almost famous

And what would happen in a movie of my life? Episodes like this. If you're reading, Ms Chastain, I suggest taking notes.

I've already mentioned how much flirting goes on between male stars and female reporters. Both parties would never declare that it's the *only* reason they do their job, but I don't think either would deny that it's a big perk. Being a story-breaking journalist or a Number 1-reaching pop star are both great things – but the power of a seductive glance is always welcome icing on the cake, whoever you are.

If things have never gone any further with a star then it's not entirely because I haven't wanted it to. There was a time when I had fewer morals and was totally prepared to be less than professional. Who wouldn't want to follow through, when single and faced with a charming movie star making eyes at you?

It had been another long week of premieres and album launches. I was enjoying a few minutes' respite while waiting in a posh hotel to interview a male film star – let's call him Chris – who was over from America to promote his latest effort (an ill-advised foray into comedy – not his greatest strength). I was feeling pretty worn out and depressed that afternoon. Seeing the same old faces in these junket waiting rooms over the years

– faces I'd probably seen more than those of my own family – can have that effect.

My outfit for this occasion reflected my mood: grey. When my name was finally called by the PR girl, I began what was by then a well-practised routine. We walked down the corridor, stopping outside the interview room where I was told to loiter for another few minutes as the chat inside was wound up. Familiar territory. These were motions I'd been through so many times before I could do them on autopilot. I sat staring absentmindedly at the flock wallpaper across from me, which probably cost more per roll than I earned per week. Hideous, I thought. Then, suddenly, a face popped round the door and snapped me out of my trance.

'Hey! You must be Holly. How are you doing today?'

He held out his hand for me to shake. I grabbed it, trying not to show my confusion at his appearance. You see, here was a guy who looked quite a lot like Chris the actor, the man I was about to interview. True, his face was certainly thinner, as was his hair. But his eyes sparkled at me in just the way Chris's did in the poster for the movie he was promoting. Maybe that picture had just caught him in a better light? Or maybe he'd since lost weight for a role?

Or maybe this guy in front of me was actually just Chris's slightly-less-good-looking older brother.

'I'm Mike, Chris's big bro. We travel everywhere together. You wanna come in now? I love your outfit today, by the way.'

Though Mike might not have been the looker in the family, his bubbliness was unusually charming on a day that had so far been unexceptional. I liked him and his ordinariness – not something you find much of in Hollywood. As I followed Mike into the interview room my dark mood was finally clearing.

And things got even better. Sitting in the middle of the suite was Chris, a man who immediately made me feel 15 again.

Admittedly, he no longer looked exactly as he had when I was one of his many teen fans, but that was no bad thing. Now he looked even better; manlier and wiser, he still nevertheless had the boyish grin that made my knees feel so jelly-like I was glad I was offered a seat. When he casually touched one of those knees during the interview – somehow managing to seem more gentlemanly than pervy – I didn't think I'd ever be able to walk again.

'We should get Holly a ticket to the premiere party tonight,' Chris called over to Mike as I was reluctantly packing away my recording gear ten minutes later. Mike . . . I'd completely forgotten he was even in the room. I felt slightly sorry for him, the hanger-on only able to taste the luxuries of success by being his brother's assistant.

'Great idea,' Mike responded from the corner of the room, before reaching into his jacket pocket and pulling out an envelope for me.

'See you there I hope!' Chris beamed at me, as I hurriedly grabbed the ticket on my way out. I knew, shamefully, that I'd not shown Mike as much gratitude as I probably should have done; he must be used to it, though, I thought. Not being jealous of a more successful family member must be tough, but accepting it and even having a laugh about it must surely be the healthiest way to cope. You might remember those adverts that featured Doug Pitt, Brad's brother, showing us around his pretty-average suburban home with all the glee of someone showing off their Hollywood mansion on MTV's *Cribs*. Doug knew that he would always be compared to his megastar brother and obviously decided to work with that rather than fight it (and get paid for promoting Virgin Mobile in the process). I was hoping that Mike had the same attitude. He was undoubtedly sweet, but Chris was obviously the one everyone wanted to hang out with – fame is an extremely intoxicating drug.

I clutched the envelope like it was one of Willy Wonka's golden tickets. Thankfully, this had been my last job of the day, so I went straight home to plan what I would wear for the party. What did I have in my wardrobe that would impress a movie star? After showering, blow-drying my hair, painting my nails and dousing my body in perfume, I flipped through the rails. This was the perfect night for a *slightly*-slutty-in-the-wrong-circumstances little red dress.

The party was being held at an old church in the centre of town. Recently refurbished, it was now hired out as a performance space and event venue for media corporations with more money than sense. Tonight, as a girl who'd had a crap week at work and even more crap six months on the dating circuit, I was grateful for that kind of expenditure. The party was spectacular, extravagantly lit and sprinkled with waiters who were plying guests with free booze at every opportunity. This was just what I needed.

Unfortunately, when it comes to parties, the occasion can be as opulent as a royal wedding, but if you don't know anyone there it will be the loneliest place in the world. I must have spent at least an hour repeatedly circling the room; refilling my glass every time I saw the bar like I was passing 'Go' and collecting £200 on a Monopoly board. By the time I finally bumped into Mike and Chris I was more drunk than Paris Hilton trying to parallel park.

'Here she is!'

Mike's gaunt face lit up when he saw me. I raised my glass and gave a surprisingly laddish response: 'Wa-hey!'

Both guys were now suited and booted, Chris looking even more suave and sexy than he had been in the hotel room that afternoon. My inhibitions by now long diluted in a lake of bubbly, I put my hand on his arm and attempted a seductive Joey-from-*Friends* style 'How *you* doing?'

He smiled weakly, his eyes not meeting mine as he looked

around the room twitchily. The guy that had paid me so much attention earlier now looked entirely distracted.

'Okay, Mike. I'm just gonna go back to the VIP. You okay now you've found her?'

'Sure, Bro. Catch you later.'

And with a brotherly fist pump, Chris was gone. I was confused. We'd been together for barely 30 seconds. Mike, on the other hand, was going nowhere. He touched my bare shoulder and smiled at me.

'For the second time today, may I say how much I love your outfit?'

I turned my gaze away from Chris's disappearing figure, and looked up at Mike's face. It was clear which of the two was interested in me. Chris could have anyone he wanted, from models to princesses. How had I thought he would fancy a humble journalist? His not-quite-so-hot close relative, on the other hand . . . Mike had probably had his fair share of liaisons because of his connections, but at the same time, lacking the potent charisma of his sibling, he punched at a different weight. And I was his next contender.

So *that's* how he dealt with his brother's fame.

Mike and I chatted. I don't know whether it was his genuinely sweet personality or the alcohol but he got progressively more attractive as the night went on. Certainly, from the right angle, I noticed that he looked enough like Chris to be kind of sexy. Slowly, I became unexpectedly grateful that Chris had abandoned us. So much so, in fact, that at around one in the morning Mike got us a car back to the hotel in which we'd met, and we spent a night together that, while not the one I had initially wanted, was enough to give a frustrated singleton a boost for a few weeks. When I woke up the next morning, in a suite almost identical to the one I'd done the interview in a day earlier, I was greeted by the sun streaming through the window on to the walls – walls clad in a ridiculously expensive flock – and by no regrets.

Mike and I exchanged some sweet emails over the following months before things petered out. I was fine with that. It was what it was, and things never got awkward. I'm still a coward, though. I know that if his brother comes back to the UK to promote another film I'll be begging a colleague do the interview instead of me. Meeting famous people can be intimidating enough. Meeting famous people that you thought fancied you, but then you realised it was actually their older brother that was interested and so you got drunk and slept with him, takes work-place embarrassment to a whole new level.

Press conferences

I've lost count of the number of films and TV shows I've seen where press conferences are depicted as rowdy, free-for-alls; a maelstrom of shouting and waving arms.

If only it were that exciting.

Press conferences, aka 'pressers', are always chaired by someone – often a journalist – whose primary job it is to keep order. They make sure that everyone puts their hand up politely if they want to get a question in, and that off-limits topics are swiftly skated over. Any troublemakers who fancy their chances with a cheeky quip are quickly dealt with in a headmaster-like way and calm is restored. These chairpersons also have to rephrase any oddball questions from the foreign press that have got slightly lost in translation. There are usually plenty. I'll always cherish the sheer surrealism of the moment when one such host had to work out exactly what it was an Asian reporter was trying to ask Robert Pattinson. The *Twilight* star looked baffled and blank until this exasperated invigilator, with the help of the audience, finally understood. 'So, Robert,' he said with a sigh. 'I think what Mariko really wants to know is: what's your favourite biscuit?'

If you already have a plan in your head for the angle you want your subsequent article to take, then asking a carefully sculpted question at one of these events is a useful way of filling in the gaps. You can almost put words into the stars' mouths. For many, though – particularly the aged and disillusioned hacks, who shuffle into the room looking more knackered than Lindsay Lohan's car bumper – a press conference is a lazy way of getting lots of material for zero effort. It's always the same guys, too, bottom feeders who set up their tape recorders on the front table, hit record, then put up their feet back in row 12 for the next half an hour as enthusiastic reporters do all the hard work. Of course, what these cheeky gits know is that, at the end of the day, everyone leaves the press conference with the same answers. They get the same share of material and can use whatever they want, without having even opened their gob. Okay, I can't deny that there's been the odd occasion when I've been sent to a very dull presser and done this myself. At three o'clock on a rainy Wednesday afternoon, it really is difficult to care what Jason Derülo thinks about life, fashion and the latest series of *The X Factor*. It's so much easier to just sit back, let everyone else do the hard work and lazily stare at that thin line of hair Jason's got around his jaw (I think it's meant to be a beard). But, it's not a good habit to get into.

So, there's the downside. In a presser it's virtually impossible to get an exclusive because everything is shared. If – and it's a big if – the talent does say something newsworthy, you know that everyone else in the room has cottoned on to it too; it then becomes a race against time as to who can get the story online or on-air first.

For the stars, press conferences are an easy way to give an interview to 50 different outlets at the same time. I'm sure if they could, most celebs would choose the press-conference route over the junket every time. It's quicker, less intimate and, with publicists circling the room and band mates or co-stars up on the stage with you, there's a real feeling of safety in numbers for the stars.

Celebrities know that it takes some serious balls for a journalist to stand up in front of a huge crowd and ask a controversial question.

It does happen, though. Personally, I've never had the necessary *cojones* to mention an off-limits subject (and, as a woman who spends a serious amount of time in leggings, I wouldn't really want them either). I have, however, sat aghast as fellow hacks essentially sign their own death warrant by posing banned questions to a shocked celeb sat a few yards away from them. If I've never again seen the reporter who stood up in front of a packed press conference and asked Guy Ritchie, at the time of being Mr Madonna, what he thought of the films of Madge's first husband Sean Penn then it's not a surprise. Then there was the Turkish reporter who for some reason felt the need to tell George Clooney that he thought his latest film was 'boring'. I'll be honest and say that I actually agreed with them (it was a very slow and intense science fiction film called *Solaris*), but would I have said it to the star in front of a crowd? I don't think so. There's more chance of me swapping my clutch for a bumbag. That guy certainly had to have some guts to have spoken his mind, but why bite the hand that feeds? Journalists who openly don't care what other people think of them soon find that publicists openly don't care whom they ban from all future press conferences.

Sarah Jessica Parker

I have confused feelings about Sarah Jessica Parker.

Like many people, I have what I'd call a 'love/hate relationship' with her most famous character, Carrie Bradshaw. Okay, so the clothes, shoes and men she's got her hands on in *Sex and the City* are pretty amazing, and ten years ago I dreamt of having her writer's lifestyle, gazing out of the window of my Manhattan apartment as I searched for inspiration for my latest article (just never question how she managed to afford it on a journalist's wage . . .). Yet, there was always something vaguely irritating about her too. The endless self-analysis, the shameless materialism and that constant obsession with prancing around her apartment in her bra and knickers to show us what a great body she's got. If it wasn't so bad in the indulgent noughties, in these tougher times of austerity it seriously grates. The press were always so obsessed with Carrie, much more so than sensible Charlotte or practical Miranda, that I don't think I ever had the guts to admit that this supposed icon was also somewhat unlikeable. Now, though, I'll happily say it.

However, away from the Manolos and Central Park skylines, Carrie and her friends offer a pretty spot-on insight into what female bonds are like for millions of us.

All of which is playing on my mind as I wait to meet the woman herself. She's had such success with *Sex and the City* that I'm struggling to remember that Sarah *isn't actually Carrie*. Indeed, she could well be nothing like her. I'm really going to have to stop myself from getting into a debate with SJP about all the issues I have with her most famous role. She is, after all, in London to promote a new film, and not her old TV show. As I look over my notes in the waiting room, I pray to the great God of Showbiz: *For pity's sake, don't let me call her Carrie.*

As the minutes tick by I find myself glancing absentmindedly around the junket waiting room and notice that there's something different about it today. While I'm aware that my career is more popular with women than men, the room is nevertheless especially full of females this morning. Like, *only* women. What's more, these women are all dolled-up to the nines. The clothes rails in Topshop must have been barren after this lot had been in there. I'm reminded of the summer of 2008 when gangs of girly mates were getting glammed up just to go to the cinema and watch the *Sex and the City* movie. But the worst thing is, I realise that I'm part of this whole charade. I think back to getting dressed that morning: I *did* spend a little extra time choosing just the right outfit. I certainly wasn't this careful yesterday when I was scheduled to interview Fern Britton. So, I'm obviously not the only one struggling to separate Sarah from her alter ego. It seems like we all want to be the one that Queen Carrie deems the most stylish. The bathroom is getting used way more than usual as we each nip in to check our lipstick and hair in a bid to look all sophisticated and Fifth Avenue. My heels are already killing me, but there's no chance of taking them off in favour of the ballet pumps I've got in my bag. After all, I think: *Carrie wouldn't.*

'Stop it Holly! She's not Carrie Bradshaw!' I tell myself. I'm relieved when a PR girl – is it just me or is even *she* looking extra groomed today? – calls out my name. I'm up next. Finally I can get away from the pack.

In the interview room, SJP looks petite, demure and stylish, but not in an intimidating way. Best of all, she's smiling. She greets me with a 'Hello, I'm Sarah', which lacks any of that whiny insecurity that I find so grating in Carrie. Quickly, thankfully, I start to relax. I'm also pleased that she's reiterated her name, just to get it into my thick skull.

The familiar game of interview tennis starts up – I serve up my questions, her answers fly back over the net. It's tricky to pack much into four minutes and we're virtually done by the time she's told me about the research she did for this role. It's hardly revelatory, but it's enough for the website that I'm working for and, crucially, I'm starting to feel extremely fond of this woman, who's been in my life for so long but towards whom I've held distinctly mixed feelings.

The interview winds up and, after a friendly shaking of hands, I head out. SJP is shouting out to me:

'Great to meet you! And I love your blouse!'

I'm on top of the world.

'Aww, thanks, Carrie. Have a good day!'

I saunter out into the corridor, beaming. It's always nice to have your impression of someone change for the better. Maybe I could even rewatch some old *Sex and the City* episodes, and find Carrie less confusing now?

'Carrie' . . . 'Carrie' . . . The name sounds so familiar, as if I'd just been saying it out loud. Hang on a minute. Shit! 'Carrie'?! Had I really just called Sarah Jessica Parker 'Carrie'?! That thing I told myself that I really *shouldn't* do?

I go over our final few words in my head, desperate to prove myself wrong. But I can't. I'd definitely used the 'C' word.

I can't go back into the room and apologise, because the next interview has already started. Instead, I hurry to the lift, desperate to get out of the hotel before anyone can talk to me about my epic fail. Thankfully, I don't have to wait long – the double doors soon slide open. A girl I know from another showbiz website steps out, looking more like a catwalk model than a computer nerd.

'Hey Holly! How did it go with SJP?'

'Oh, fine, fine.' I'm edging into the lift, trying to escape.

'Fab. It must be hard not to call her Carrie, right? I did that once, with Jennifer Aniston. Called her Rachel. God, I looked such an idiot. Everyone in the interview room was cracking up. I've never felt so stupid. *Love* your blouse, by the way!'

'Okay then. Bye!'

The doors close and I'm free. Awkward as that conversation was, I'm feeling a lot better – this inability to separate actors from the characters they play clearly troubles everyone. It doesn't help that, even when actresses like Parker and Aniston are playing different characters than the ones they're most famous for, there are often inherent similarities. Great as they are at what they do, they aren't 'chameleon' actors like Christian Bale or Meryl Streep, who method act and manipulate their bodies to become a totally different person. I've seen a lot of Jen's movies and nine times out of ten I'd struggle to tell you how her character differs from that of Rachel Green. No doubt both actresses could play many different roles, but they're still so synonymous with a single character that they've become typecast, and moving on will always be difficult – not least because there are dipsticks like me who continue to get confused.

I'm interviewing Robert Pattinson about his new, non-*Twilight*, film in a few weeks. Forget dressing up to look chic this time. I'll be rocking the much geekier 'marker pen on hand look', four words tattooed on to my palm so that I don't make another mistake: Don't Call Him Edward.

Boy bands

Boy bands can be horny little buggers – and they don't try to hide it. Sometimes I think that, if you took their songs away from them, you'd basically just be left with five randy builders.

Don't just take my word for it. 5ive, I'm sure you know, were a big deal in the charts in the late nineties, scoring three Number 1 singles and endless press coverage. They were one of Simon Cowell's early success stories. Cocky in the extreme, interviewing 5ive was always a demanding experience, albeit an enjoyable one. So when Abs from the band (now rather brilliantly known as Abz) recently admitted to having slept with between 500 and 1,000 girls, most of which were teenage groupies, I wasn't shocked that he'd done it, only that he had to guess *somewhere in a 500 woman range*. That's quite a margin of difference there, Abz. Robbie Williams's autobiography *Feel*, meanwhile, catalogues numerous fan flings, including one night in which Rob bedded two Westlife fans he met in a bar. Sleeping with your own groupies is one thing, but pulling another act's is apparently even better.

The kind of playfulness we're used to seeing in boy bands today has, I'm sure, been around for ever, but it's only recently that they've become so open about it. Boy band members used to have to keep that kind of behaviour under wraps; now, it seems, the more of a player you are the better. Certainly, the very first boy bands that I interviewed, whatever they were getting up to in their personal lives, played it very safe for the press.

First there was Boyzone. When I met the Irish five piece, they were at a seaside resort doing some promo for a fizzy drink – an example of just what celebrities will do for money – and I was dispatched up there to get an interview. Okay, so even Harry Styles would find it difficult to be charming while strapped into a roller coaster, let alone give coherent answers to my questions, but still, my overriding memory of that day was at the subsequent reception where lead singer Ronan Keating serenaded the town's white-haired old-lady Mayor with an impromptu version of 'Father and Son'. Hardly the behaviour of a naughty boy. Ronan might have gone on to have a fling with a backing dancer that would eventually end his 14-year-long marriage, but in the public eye you'd have struggled to find someone more saintly.

The Backstreet Boys – my next conquests – would, I believed, be different. Formed in early nineties Florida by showbiz impresario Lou Pearlman, a man so respectable that he's currently serving prison time for – among other things – money laundering, it's easy to forget that back in the day BSB were successfully sold to the teenage masses as lovable rogues, dangerous teen hip-hoppers from the wrong side of the tracks. If Boyzone were nice Irish lads who sang Bee Gees cover versions and loved their mammies, Backstreet Boys were supposedly cheeky urban teens who wore their baseball caps back to front and sang lines like 'Jam on coz Backstreet's got it'. I say 'supposedly'; AJ's real name was Alexander and B-Rock was christened Brian. Hardly threatening. But that was the image, one that had been working brilliantly for several months when, on one of their rare visits to the UK, I was sent to a TV studio to get an interview with these young rebels.

In reality, these guys took themselves so seriously you'd think they were The Beatles rather than the group of pretty boys who belted out 'Everybody (Backstreet's Back)'. I was bitterly disappointed, since I'd long held a secret crush on Kevin Richardson from the group, a chisel-jawed man who was clearly about ten years older than his colleagues. The most light-hearted of the quintet, Brian Littrell and Nick Carter, giggled throughout the whole interview like those awful cartoon idiots Beavis and Butthead. Hardly twinkle-eyed charmers. I blamed jet lag for their monosyllabic answers (after all, who wouldn't be knackered after endless touring?). As I left the studio, wondering how to make these guys sound vaguely interesting, I was met by a crowd of fans waiting outside the building in the evening sun, hemmed in by burly bouncers and watching me leave:

'Look at that girl. She's got tape recorder. Oi! Lady! You just met Backstreet Boys, yeah?'

'Er, yes. Yes I have.'

'Oh my God! Oh my God! Is you famous?'

'No. I'm just a reporter.'

'But you just met Backstreet Boys. What's Nick like? He's so fit.'

'Well, to be honest, he was just a bit boring. Didn't really have much to say. The same with all of them actually.'

'You what? You don't know what you're talking about. What do you know, yeah?'

I continued up the road to the sound of expletive-filled catcalls from a hundred angry teenage girls, all desperate to break free from their pen and slap me.

But there was a turning point. A few years ago the various

trysts in the lives of One Direction would have been hidden from the public, the boys being forced to look 'single' so as not to put off their fans from fancying them. Now we know pretty much everything about everyone that Harry's dated, with his image as a playboy apparently only enhancing his reputation rather than destroying it.

The first time I noticed this change was with Blue. These guys didn't try to hide their laddy ways, either in their music, heavily influenced by seductive American R'n'B, or in their interviews. It didn't matter that they weren't exactly Brains of Britain. ('You should have been sent a form,' I found myself explaining to one of them on the day of a General Election, after he'd admitted to having no idea how to vote.) The Blue boys lived to flirt, hyperactively randy terriers who seemed they'd just as soon dry hump your leg as talk about their music. To be honest, I loved interviewing them. I don't think I'm special – my fellow female reporters would all say exactly the same thing about the boys' flirtiness, I'm sure. The truth is, if you're a straight guy who really cares about music then you'll probably form a rock-influenced band in the hopes of being taken seriously. If you voluntarily join a boy band, on the other hand, you're probably not in it just for the credibility. You're in it for the girls.

Interviews with boy bands now frequently descend into playground high jinks, with the guys joking around and winding you up – the equivalent of the little boy pulling the pigtails of the girl he fancies in class. Trying to pick coherent sentences out of the interview when you're back in front of your computer is an almost impossible task. But the teen audience love it. Young girls lap up that kind of mucking about. When you're 14, you're probably too afraid to go out with such scamps in real life (and it'd probably be a nightmare if you did). Worshipping one in a boy band from afar, however, is an enticingly safer prospect.

Interviewing boy bands is undeniably fun, so I for one don't mind if they seem to be only after one thing. Let's be honest, I doubt I'd have as many laughs with Radiohead.

Old Rockers

Great rock stars don't have to put on an act. They're like that the whole time. While blokey guitar music isn't exactly my preferred listening, I've always admired the crinkly old-timers who just live and breathe their profession. Ozzy Osbourne, Ronnie Wood, Lemmy – these guys seem more pickled than the jar of beetroot I've got sitting in my cupboard, but at least they've got no side to them. They are what they are, honest and unaffected. Behaving as if you're in your twenties when you're actually an OAP looks pretty sad when most people try it. (Exhibit A: Peter Stringfellow.) But when you found fame back in the day as the coolest kid on the music scene, why would you see any point in trying to change? If it ain't broke, why fix it? They're the original bad boys.

Alexandra Burke is an unlikely philosopher, but when she sang 'the bad boys are always catching my eye' I knew exactly where she was coming from. When it comes to interviews, the bad boys (I realise the phrase is hardly cutting edge but if it's good enough for Alex . . .) are always the more fun ones. They've been there and done that and don't give a shit about saying the 'right' thing any more. That's no doubt a nightmare for their publicists but it's a dream come true for us journalists. Score an interview with a self-styled rebel and you're more than likely to come out with a cutting comment on a co-star or controversial soundbite on world events. These chaps don't do 'autopilot'.

Take Liam Gallagher. I certainly relish watching him grow old disgracefully. Grabbing a soundbite from the former Oasis lead singer never fails to keep you on your toes, too. He's enjoyably unpredictable. If you're stood in the press pen at the BRIT Awards and he swishes by, shouting out one of his trademark bluff Northerner one-liners, then it always adds a bit of colour to an often stuffy evening. His joy is that he doesn't seem to have any filter on his thoughts; what is conjured up in his head comes straight out of his mouth, untouched by manners or moderation. Great fun.

Some favourite slices of Gallagher wit include:

'Posh boys can't take drugs, man. They're lightweights. They have one little line and they're in rehab.'

'Chris Martin looks like a Geography teacher.'

'Victoria Beckham? She can't even chew gum and walk in a straight line, let alone write a book.'

'Spongebob Squarepants – he's the f****** man!'

Despite a certain lack of finesse, I find it hard to disagree with much of what he's saying! Follow @LiamGQuotes on Twitter if you fancy a regular supply of Britpop one-liners.

There is a downside to this type of guitar-wielding man's man, though. If you're writing a bigger feature and need something *a little more* than just attitude and swearing, it can be a struggle. Admiring rock gods on-stage or on a red carpet is great but a lot of these wild men, it seems, don't do 'deeper insight'.

Sit down with Liam for longer than a minute and his iconic swagger can suddenly become quite irritating. Every perfectly reasonable question is batted back to you with a Mancunian snarl as if it's the most ridiculous thing that he's ever heard, while any vaguely coherent sentence he utters is usually littered with so much swearing you know there's a long night of editing ahead of you. Can he really go through daily life with that kind of posturing? Imagine buying a pint of milk from Sainsbury's while pogoing around with the aggression of a prize fighter? I'm certain that deep down there's someone with interesting things to say. But despite all the machismo he just doesn't seem man enough to say them.

I'll continue to admire these hard-living geezers, though. In a world of shameless publicity and quickfire fame, they're reliably curmudgeonly and true-to-their-word. But while I understand how the whole point of being a rebellious rock star is that actions speak louder than words, that's not much use if you've got to sit down for ten minutes and have a serious interview with the old git.

No personal questions

I can't claim to always be a perfectly moral journalist. Getting the story – sometimes by any means necessary – is an intoxicating process, and when you're on the scent, good manners are sometimes the last thing you think about.

Still, I've seen the paparazzi chasing someone down the street and it's not something I'd wish upon my worst enemy. I'm not one to criticise celebrities for wanting their privacy. There's an old argument that such treatment is just part of the deal if you seek fame, but I'm mellowing as I get older and I can see now that even an A-Lister deserves their downtime. When they're in work mode – at a premiere, doing a gig – that's fair enough, but outside of that? It's like walking home at night after a hard day's work only to be greeted by everyone from the office on the doorstep, waiting to have a meeting. There's a time and place for everything. If celebs use the media when they want to promote something, yet shun it when they want peace and quiet, is that really so bad? No one likes having to work overtime.

Nevertheless, there is such a thing as being too cagey. A phrase I hear all too often these days – certainly more than when I started as a journalist – is 'no personal questions allowed'. All too often these blanket bans are less to do with a celebrity's privacy, and more about their publicist who probably just wants to justify their own existence. By making their movie star or pop singer client clam up, they're actually doing them more harm than good.

Take the time that I met Justin Timberlake. I'd always had plenty of time for him, having watched him grow from boy band eye candy into a respected solo star, more than replicating the success of Robbie Williams and George Michael, but in that cool American way that makes it all seem so natural and easy. And unlike these British counterparts, JT hadn't had to endure the scandal of rehab and car crashes and, er, you know the rest. Everyone seemed to like him – a rare thing in showbiz.

Justin was in town to promote a film, his music career at this point reduced to just a few guest appearances on tracks rather than entire solo albums. Such an about turn was a bold move for a singer who'd sold 20 million records, but his acting seemed better than many who'd done similar things (yeah, I'm talking about you Mariah). The atmosphere in the waiting room at the junket was, thus, full of goodwill. Until, that is, a pen-pusher low down in the ranks of Justin's entourage came into the waiting room and, with a nonchalance only PR people can pull off, delivered 'the line'.

'I just wanted to make it clear, Justin won't be answering any questions about music. Mmmmkay?'

'Er . . . sorry?'

'Justin Timberlake—'

'Yes, I know who he is.'

'Well, he only wants to talk about being an actor, not his music.'

'Right. So the guy who made his name as a musician, sold millions of records as a musician, is globally loved and respected as a musician, doesn't want to talk about being a musician.'

'No.'

'Rrrrright.'

The blanket ban didn't go down well with my colleagues, many of whom were only at the junket because they worked for music magazines and websites, and so were obviously interested in one of the biggest names in the music industry. Immediately the mood changed from one of excitement to trepidation. Anyone who makes demands as to what they can and can't be asked must be hard work, we reasoned – especially when the taboo topic actually seemed entirely harmless. I wonder if, now he's back in musician mode, finally releasing his third album after a seven-year break, you're not allowed to ask him about his experiences acting? When I find out, I'll tell you . . .

Eventually my time comes and I approach the interview room with a shrug of the shoulders, a heavy heart and solid plans to donate my CD of *Justified* to the charity shop.

I didn't ask about the music, of course. I knew better. And, as it turns out, Justin was sweet and modest (and wearing glasses, as if to prove his new status as a serious thespian). My four minutes done I left the hotel with an interview that was decent, if lacking in any information about a huge chunk of his career. Yet, because of that demand, my memory of him has been tainted. I mean, really, what would have been so bad about asking him about his music? Asking him about Britney Spears, a girl with whom he'd had a teenage relationship ten years earlier and presumably had left way in his past, would have been stupid and pointless. Asking him about his favourite sexual position with Jessica Biel, also probably a question too far. But his massively successful music career? Could he not have just said: 'Oh well, thanks for the interest, Holly, but I'm kinda concentrating on movies at the moment. I'm sure there'll be another record someday'? Chattiness and charm are always preferable to stony silence. It's as if publicists don't trust their talent to be able to handle such spectacular improvisation.

There has to be some common sense involved. I didn't bat an

eyelid when, just before a press conference with a massive female pop star, we were all told 'no personal questions'. With rumours in the press about her relationship with both a married actor and a questionable ex there was potential scandal in her love life that I'm sure she didn't want to get bogged down in. I can understand that. And really, if you're a showbiz journalist and think that a star is going to reveal their innermost secrets to a room full of hacks just because you asked them to then you must be pretty stupid (although someone actually did ask her about her love life – they quickly found themselves on the end of a scary superstar glare and a bollocking from the organisers).

But not *every* question that delves outside of what the talent is promoting should be deemed dodgy. Common sense tells us that some topics are, in the grand scheme of things, pretty harmless and are better handled with a quip and a smile by the star, rather than just looking pissed off. It's in all our interests. They don't look stroppy and we go back to work with an answer, even if it's not the most revelatory response of all time. Everyone wins.

I really wish the team behind Cameron Diaz, one of my favourite actresses, famous for her down-to-earth approach to life, had felt like that. Just as I was about to go in to the interview room, a flunky pounced on me with the classic 'No personal questions' routine. I looked at my notes and mentally scrubbed out at least half of what I'd planned to ask. As Cameron had just started dating someone new – a relationship that was very much out in the open – I'd hoped to have a casual chat with her about it. She always gave off a happy, friendly vibe, so why not? Now my plans had been scuppered. In the end, the interview went well, even if I struggled to think of questions related to the silly comedy she was promoting (even Paxman would've struggled with that task). But, once again, I found myself wondering why someone as utterly charming as her couldn't have been allowed to banter with me about boyfriends rather than shutting down completely. She certainly had the ability. But no . . . the publicist had made their decision and a chance for their client to actually look cool rather than just plain cold had been missed.

And the identity of Cameron's then squeeze, he-whose-name-was-not-to-be-mentioned?

Justin Timberlake, of course.

Personal questions . . . please!

It's mid-morning, and I'm still in my pyjamas, working from home. The piece I have to write today is about Robbie Williams – a quick list of some of his career highs and lows that I was told wouldn't need to be that long. I'm not so sure, though. Good old Robbie has been up and down more often than Russell Brand's Y-fronts. What's more, he doesn't try to hide it:

'Robbie blames flop album for feeling "lethargic and depressed"'

'Robbie: "I'd have died from drugs if I hadn't checked into rehab"'

'"I'm loving aliens instead" Robbie thinks they've invaded his home . . .'

'Robbie: "I tried to stab myself when high on LSD"'

The headlines tell you everything you need to know. Robbie likes to share. His life has been spoken about so much, largely by him, it's going to be difficult to keep this piece under novel length. I can't complain though. Major stars that are happy to reveal their problems are the holy grail of showbiz reporting. While benefiting from someone else's problems might not be the most morally sound thing a showbiz reporter can do, I'm finding that it's happening more and more now.

You see, with so many celebs now going through emotional

breakdowns at some point in their careers – the glare of the spotlight more blinding than ever these days – there's a strong chance that when you're innocently chatting to one of them at an event or party they're on the brink of one right there and then. It's become a frightening norm. What's more, where many stars used to keep these personal problems hidden, loads now seem to use interviews as some kind of therapy in itself, unburdening themselves of their demons while the reporter sits next to them mentally rubbing their hands with glee. It's not something every star does, of course. Accidentally ask Rihanna about Chris and you'll immediately get the silent treatment. It's certainly true to say, however, that extreme honesty has become more popular than ever.

Robbie Williams was one of my first experiences of this open approach. I'd grown up loving him as the prankster in Take That, the cheeky one whose attempts to shed his boy band image in the nineties resulted in drink and drug misuse, a stint in rehab and the kind of ill-advised bleached blonde hairdo that you only attempt when you're off your face. He certainly wasn't the first pop star to party hard, but the extent to which it was publicised – a lot of which was fuelled by his own openness and honesty – was a real surprise. Every time you turned on your tape recorder around Robbie, he was sure to reference his problems. His approach was the very opposite to 'no personal questions'.

We couldn't believe our luck.

Addictions to alcohol, cigarettes, drugs (illegal and prescription) and even Lucozade; it seems that Robbie had them all and was fine with talking about them too. Coincidentally, as his star rose that of another singing sensation – Michael Jackson – was rapidly waning, the American singer's life a confusing bunch of rumours about his own issues and illnesses. Michael himself was rarely interviewed and even when he was, would deny the stories with an increasingly unbelievable bunch of excuses. Thus two megastars' lives had many parallels, but were dealt with in completely contradictory ways. Everyone knew Robbie had problems because he didn't stop talking about them.

It never felt like he was merely looking for sympathy though. He's far too self-aware for that. I genuinely believe that when Robbie wants to reveal all about his life it's for no other reason than a no-nonsense, typically North-of-England approach of 'Why not?'

Why pay a fortune to Californian therapists when you can just chat to whichever person happens to be sat next you at the time?

Thankfully Robbie's long since come out the other side, a happily married man and father. Those wild days, however, still echo in everything he says, even today. Content in adult life, he's still not a man who wants to hide his feelings. So while he might have you laughing one minute at his hyperactivity and showmanship, you know that they mask a dark past that must have been hell for him and his family. All of which, let's be honest, makes for a great interview. I can't feel ashamed, though. When someone seems so keen to talk about their problems, why should I?

On the other hand, I probably shouldn't agree to sum them up in just 250 words.

The good, the bad, and the interview

It was a Friday morning in May and I wasn't having a great time with Avril Lavigne.

She's probably grown up a bit now but when I met the 'Sk8er Boi' singer those few years back she was sitting with her hands in her pockets and hoody over her head, mumbling like a surly schoolgirl on detention after being caught smoking behind the Chemistry lab (having once been that girl, I can empathise). It was a warm, cloudless day in Dublin (where Avril was about to kick off the second European leg of her world tour), but the young singer was behaving as if she was a character from *Twilight*, afraid of the sun.

When asked for insight into her music and set-list, she had none: 'Huh . . . like . . . I just do what I wanna. That's it.'

When asked for thoughts on her hobbies and personal life, she had none of those either:

'Er . . . like . . . Just the normal stuff. Music, movies, y'know.'

I was seriously struggling.

If I was asked to name the toughest interview I've ever done, it would be this one. Having since spent a lot of time going over it in my head, I think I'm closer to understanding why it was so difficult, though. In her defence, Avril's rise to fame hadn't been as smooth as it might have seemed to the public. The pop-punk sound that we associate with her wasn't initially appreciated by the money men controlling her music career and she spent a year pre-fame being forced to record Shania Twain-esque ballads to fit in with their plans. Twelve months of Country and Western would scar anyone for life. When it became clear that Avril's heart wasn't into being a teen cowgirl, she headed to California to find herself. With her subsequent rock album *Let Go* shifting 17 million copies, it's safe to say that she didn't need to look that hard (and I'm sure those tone deaf bosses found themselves liking her girly punk sound a whole lot more once the royalty cheques came rolling in).

So while I'm never going to describe Avril as the bubbliest person in music, I can appreciate that she'd probably already had enough of people wanting her to be a certain way by the time I met her. Eight months into her world tour she was probably also exhausted. I ploughed on with my smiley questioning, feeling like a square teacher trying to get a problem pupil enthusiastic about Shakespeare. In the end I wrapped up the proceedings early, admitting defeat. I guessed if I really wanted to find out about Avril's emotions it'd be better to listen to her confessional lyrics than to expect her to open up with a microphone under her nose.

It's certainly true that pop stars are tougher to interview than actors simply because they often want their songs to speak for themselves (it's also a lot easier to talk about the plot of a movie than the sound of an album). Still, I suddenly felt sorry for my own parents, bringing up the moody teenage me who wouldn't have a conversation with anyone but who filled up endless notepads with pained sixth form poetry. Teenage stars are great news stories, that's for sure. However, just like when they're your own children, they can be bloody hard work.

Asking me to name the *easiest* interview is actually much harder.

You see, thankfully, most people are nice. The majority of performers get into the spotlight thanks to real passion and creativity and are happy to talk about it. The person who seems to have the most fun, though, is Cameron Diaz. Put her in an interview and she's like the anti-Avril. I might have had problems with Cameron's publicity team in the past, barring me from asking about her love life, but get to the woman herself and you're faced with someone warm, funny and happy. Admittedly, if I had legs like Cameron Diaz, I'd be ecstatically happy too.

That said, I've met plenty of A-List bombshells who look a million dollars but who act as if they've got nothing to celebrate. I call it the 'pissed-off princess' syndrome – women with the kind of lives most of us would cut off a limb to have, still behaving as if the whole world is against them. Cameron Diaz, I'm pleased to say, is the polar opposite. I'm sure she does have to cut back on the Krispy Kremes to stay in such great shape, but she never behaves like someone who's miserable in her abstinence. On the contrary, Cameron radiates health, cheerfulness and a laidback attitude to life.

To be honest, this was not what I expected as I waited to meet her for the first time. On top of the 'no personal questions' bomb-shell being dropped on me by the publicists, I was also suffering from that distinctly female attitude of 'She's thin and pretty, there-fore she can't be very nice'. I'm sure you know what I mean. The friendliness that I encountered when I walked into the hotel room, however, seemed genuine, born out of a stable Hispanic family life (her paternal grandparents were Cuban immigrants) and an inherent bullshit detector that must have worked overtime in her early days. After her brilliant breakthrough alongside Jim Carrey in *The Mask*, Cameron was Hollywood's hottest new star and was offered pretty much every role under the sun. Cleverly she chose instead to hone her craft in small indie movies (she hadn't even acted prior to the Carrey movie, working instead as a model) and refused to be sucked in by the hype. The woman now speaking into my microphone, 15 years later, looked every inch a confident star who knew what she wanted. She didn't even seem to mind that London was in the grip of an especially cold and wet autumn at the time, which must have made her native San Diego seem even further away.

If I remember correctly, Cameron was rocking casual black jeans, ballet pumps and a soft grey, off-the-shoulder sweater, looking a million miles away from a high-maintenance *fashionista* she could so easily be. The more we spoke the more I realised that she's just as laddishly cheeky as she is chatty and feminine, making me feel instantly comfortable. Sitting just a few feet away from her as she unleashed that megawatt smile made me want to invite her around for a pyjama party where we'd spend the night painting our nails, watching chick flicks and talking about boys (which, of course, I *definitely* wasn't allowed to ask her about in the interview).

From what I learnt in my short encounters with her and from reading subsequent interviews with her, she sees Hollywood for what it really is, a game, and the fact she spends plenty of time away from the craziness, chilling out surfing, is the right attitude in my book. Cameron was even sorted enough to be able to co-star with her aforementioned ex, Mr Timberlake, in *Bad Teacher*.

During my second interview with Cameron, things got even better. She wasn't surrounded by her 'team' as she had been before, and she didn't bat an eyelid talking about romance. I couldn't believe it. To be honest, I was relieved. Anyone so at odds with the uptight mentality of the people scurrying around her will always get my vote. At 40, it's perhaps a bit of a shame that Cameron is still to find Mr Right. Yet, on the flip side, she doesn't seem that bothered. What's more, I don't think there's many men out there who could cope with someone who's as on top of their life as Cameron D. Emo rockers could learn a lot from her.

Interestingly, in both of these cases, I could tell whether the interview was likely to be good or bad from the moment I stepped into the room. There are certain things that give the game away, even early on. Here's a list of some tell-tale signs:

Is the interview schedule running on time? If yes, you're about to meet someone who cares what you think of them. If no, chances are they don't give a shit. And it's not just being late that should set alarm bells ringing. On occasion, the schedule can even run early, which normally means the star is giving such short, monosyllabic answers that journalists are wrapping things up ahead of schedule. Never good.

Does the celebrity look at you when you walk in the room or do they carry on a conversation with one of their entourage? If you get eye contact, you're on to a winner. If you're frozen out from the moment you come through the door, you might as well just pack up and go home.

Do they ask you your name? Of course, your answer might well go in one ear and out the other but still, being asked your name shows a politeness that always bodes well for the rest of the interview.

What's their handshake like? It's like your grandad always told you, never trust someone with a limp grip. If they don't even want to take your hand, you're on even thinner ice.

And their body language? Avril's hands-in-pockets look was certainly easy to interpret. I've even interviewed a girl band where one member was resting her head on her colleague's shoulder, sound asleep (the resulting interview was, unsurprisingly, excruciating). Open arms and comfortably sitting back in the seat are what you're ideally always after, like a couple of friends having a chat in the pub.

After hastily analysing all that in the first 30 seconds of your meeting, it's now time to actually do the interview. If you've been faced with someone who's late, limp-handed and doesn't care what you're called or about looking you in the eye, then all I can say is: Good Luck!

Beyoncé

I'm walking out of the hotel room when the distinctive voice suddenly strikes up again:

'I lahk yer payants!'

Beyoncé is calling out to me (that was my attempt at phonetically replicating her Texas accent, by the way).

'Oh ... er ... thanks,' I mumble, before I scurry out of the room like a frightened rodent. Nice move, Holly. Classy. There goes the invite to Jay-Z's birthday party.

My 'payants' that day, as I recall, had been a pair of spray-on jeans that left me gasping for breath. But since they also have the effect of 'sucking in the thighs' (my father's caring words), I squeeze myself into that denim whenever I need to look my best. Meeting Beyoncé – owner of some of the best quadriceps in the business – was definitely a thigh-sucking day.

The 'payants' quickly became known as my 'Beyoncé jeans' – my friend Danny seeming to take sadistic pleasure in encouraging me to cram into them on every occasion, as if the very fabric had once been stretched around B's own shapely derrière. Sweet, but I doubt she'd buy her Size 12s from New Look.

The 'payants' comment, however, had more to it than meets the eye. It was a classic example of a celebrity trick designed to make reporters feel like we've had a special moment. In the same way that the final five minutes of some really bad movies can be so amazing and explosive you momentarily convince yourself that the two very painful hours before this were great too, a celebrity ending an average interview with a compliment can get us leaving the room on a high. But while I've no doubt that she complimented many reporters on that afternoon, saying nice things just another of her ways of seeming to give everything while simultaneously revealing nothing, I still fell for it. I left the interview with pretty much the same bland material as everyone else, but I was smiling like I'd won the Lottery. Cunning move, Bouncy.

Don't get me wrong: I love a bit of B. I've even learnt nearly all the moves to the 'Single Ladies' dance routine (buy me enough Kir Royales and maybe I'll show you). But as the old saying goes, 'Never meet your heroes'. So while B was polite, polished and looked absolutely stunning, dare I say that she was just a teeny-*weeny* bit safe?

Perhaps because of the length of her fame, which stems back to her teens, she now seems so robotic in all the interviews I've watched that much of her (no doubt lovely) personality seems to have been erased. It's all to do with control, of course. Even the documentary about her life called *Life is but a Dream* – an 'up-close and personal' look at her career, pregnancy with Blue Ivy and earlier miscarriage – was directed by none other than . . . Beyoncé. Putting up the guard is just another way of having the final cut on your life. When you're that well known, of course, it's understandable that you'd want to be protective of your privacy, but society doesn't always react well to people who seem to be hiding something, even if they're not. The result? Rumours, such as the one about her faking her pregnancy with Blue Ivy and actually using a surrogate mother. Sometimes being in control can actually work against you.

With me – a huge fan – Beyoncé spoke plenty but said so little. I think she knew it too. She knows that it's when she's in front of a crowd – where the audience is in the palm of her hand – rather than an interviewer that she really sparkles. Watch her incredible performances on stage and she's Sasha Fierce, one of the greatest performers we've ever seen. Faced with a journalist's questions, though, and it seems she quickly morphs into Bertha Boring. Albeit a beautiful Bertha Boring who apparently *really* loved my trousers.

TV Totty

The media is full of middle-class people catering to audiences that they'd probably never mix with in real life. Most of my employers have an idea of their target consumer – the person to have in mind whenever they're putting together a piece. I've lost count of the number of times she's been referred to as 'Towerblock Tracy'. Behind the harsh nickname, though, there's a serious point: as a journalist you must always, always respect your audience. While 'Towerblock Tracy' – in her twenties, baby and boyfriend, tight budget, loves showbiz gossip – might not be the mirror image of me, it's she who ultimately pays my bills by buying the magazines I write for. To me she's the greatest person in the world.

However, while there are magazines aimed specifically at posh people – and where subsequently a lot of posh people go to work – television doesn't have quite the same class system as the press. There's no small-screen version of *Tatler* or *The Lady*.

As a result, you get shows aimed squarely at Tracy and the mass market being made by teams who probably have more interest in real operas than soap operas. That really hit home, the one and only time I've ever been on TV.

I had never wanted to be on television. I watched loads of it and admired the smart, sassy female presenters who'd made an impact in a male-dominated world (Mariella Frostrup, Janet Street-Porter, Paula Yates), but I never for a second imagined I could do their job. I had opinions, of course, but they only really formed themselves into something coherent when I was sat in front of a computer. Ask me to vocalise them and I'd more than likely turn into a stuttering buffoon – Hugh Grant in heels.

All of this is playing on my mind as I sit in the back of a chauffeured car several years later – a car taking me to the studios of a daytime TV show.

The programme in question was a magazine show, something so average that it's not even on-air any more. The producers had wanted a gossip section every week and so got in touch with an editor that I work for to offer her the gig. She was perfect for it – bubbly and brassy, but also entirely up on the latest goings on in the showbiz world. Watching her do her bit became a ritual in my living room every Wednesday morning.

Then, one week she couldn't make it and – shockingly – she suggested me to the producers as a replacement. At first I was chuffed, feeling like the teacher's pet. Then after a few minutes, panic set in. Would I fluff my lines under the pressure of live TV? And what about what my friend Danny poetically refers to as my 'potty mouth'? What if I dropped the 'F bomb' on cosy daytime telly? Finally, I became suspicious. Maybe I'd only been recommended as a replacement by my editor because she deliberately wanted someone terrible to cover for her? That way she'd seem even better when she came back.

Despite these concerns, I still said yes. 'How often do these chances come around?' I had sternly asked myself. What's more, as someone who's watched more than her fair share of daytime TV, just being able to see how it all worked would be an experience. So with a deep breath I passed on my details to the production team, carefully planned out the feature with an aloof-sounding researcher on the phone the next week, and then before I could say 'Richard and Judy', I am heading to the studio in the back of a Mercedes. I am petrified.

'I've always wanted to be best friends with TV totty,' were Erica's words of encouragement as she watched me lay half the contents of my wardrobe out on the bed that morning. That had only made me feel the pressure even more. The seemingly endless car journey to the other side of London eventually settles me a little, but as we pull up outside the studio and I'm greeted by a willowy blonde girl with a clipboard and the figure of a schoolboy, I'm tempted to get the driver to turn back. But in I go.

'Hi, I'm Tabby. I'm a runner on the show,' she says with the louche confidence of a girl whose daddy probably owned the company. 'I'll take you in to meet Toby, the researcher you've been speaking with.'

'Tabby and Toby?' I say, nervously giggling.

'Yah,' she replies, expressionless. 'Funny, right?'

Inside the corridors of the building there appear to be at least 20 Tabby clones, all sauntering about effortlessly, occasionally speaking into their Britney-style headsets while checking something on their clipboard. A ramshackle-looking lanky boy with an unironed shirt and floppy hair comes out of a sideroom and walks towards me.

'Hey, I'm Toby. Great to meet at last.'

Tabby slinks away, mumbling something into her headset as she goes. Toby continues: 'So, we're all good? I'll take you through to make-up.'

The room is a hive of activity, full of a few more Tabbys, more clipboards and more headset chatter. As the make-up girl is caking on the war paint, spending a disconcerting amount of time on the dark circles under my eyes, Toby gives me a set of cue cards, all typed up with the topics we've discussed over the phone. At least I won't be lost for words. Unfortunately, as he's running through everything I find myself becoming distracted by the other guests who are having their faces done next to me. Just a few feet away sits a glamour girl dolled up like a hooker – eyelashes so big her blinking could start a tsunami – as well as a wide-boy soap star who regularly finds himself in the tabloids. It's here that the difference between who this particular show was aimed at and who the people are that make it becomes most clear. This is posh kids making television for their cleaning ladies.

Twenty minutes later I am on-set, shaking hands with the presenters and ready to do my stint. The male presenter is very sweet; although so severely caked in fake tan I feel like I could peel it off in one go. The woman is undeniably the bigger star and I sense a bit of tension because of it. She's known for being a bit uptight and prim. As she sits there regally in her chair, he's going full pelt and slating the package that's playing out, a piece about cooking a family dinner for a fiver.

'Jesus. Just get a job and buy an M&S ready meal,' the man mumbles to himself, before turning to me and smiling. 'Okay, Holly. We'll just get this crap out of the way then it's over to you. Thirty seconds to go.'

His co-star looks at him and rolls her eyes.

Suddenly a red bulb lights up on top of one of the cameras and I see Toby smiling at me from the wings and giving the thumbs up. Suddenly the hosts are not introducing me. For the next four minutes all I have to do is laugh at this guy's bad jokes and forget that swear words even exist.

I succeed. *Just.*

'So finally then, Holly, one for us girls – Enrique Iglesias! Oooh, I say! He's just announced he's releasing his first new single in two years, hasn't he?'

'Yes, the king of Latino Pop is back. Still not married to Anna

Kournikova, though. Come on Enrique, man up and pop the question!'

'So there's a new album and a tour on the way then?'

'Definitely. You can find all the dates on your website if you fancy an evening of steamy tunes!'

'And you've heard the song, haven't you? What's it like?'

'Oh, it's fuc—'

No! No! No! I stop myself and take a gulp. How can this have happened? I'd got too comfortable. I'd been hurriedly waffling away like I do down the pub and become lost. Now I have to try to stage a last-minute comeback. Shit! Shit! Shit! No – don't say shit. Forget all swear words, Holly. Your moment is nearly over and you can swear all you like then but just for these final seconds get back on track. The presenters are looking at me, still awaiting my crucial verdict on Enrique.

'It's *far classier* than anything he's done before. Gonna be huge!'

I blurt out those last three words in a strange screech, desperately overcompensating for my earlier blip and relieved that my time is up. Actually, despite time seeming to stand still right at the end, the feature is over and done with ridiculously quickly. Until that final moment, I felt like I was only just getting into my stride. As a writer I spend hours on articles, double-page spreads with a four-figure word count that, hopefully, will be read more than once. With TV it seems that all the hard work is in the planning. The features themselves are done with in the blink of an eye.

'Okay, we're in the adverts!' shouts out the floor manager. Everyone visibly relaxes.

'I wondered what you were going to say at the end there,' the female presenter says, still a bit stiff but undeniably friendly.

I feign ignorance. 'Oh really? Why?'

'Well,' she continues, 'I just didn't think you looked like an

Enrique Iglesias fan. Interesting you think he's "classy". I think he's *fucking* awful.'

I'm in shock. Hearing that kind of language from her is like discovering the Queen has toilet breaks. You just don't expect it. Another shout rings out across the studio: 'Back in twenty!' and I'm ushered off set, leaving the two hosts to carry on with the show. Next up, a piece on synthetic hair extensions.

I've got away with it. Tabby and Toby wave me off as a car takes me back home and back to the comfort of my keyboard. I enjoyed my daytime TV experience but knew which world was for me. Television seemed like harder work for less satisfaction. The main advantage it appeared to offer was more fame and exposure than the world of writing, but those things can quickly morph into vanity. With all those public schoolers running things, it hardly seemed authentic either. My star-struck friends on the other hand, watching from work, obviously thought otherwise about my brush with broadcasting.

Minutes after I'd come off air my mobile beeped with a text from Erica: 'U were great Holls.'

One from Daisy: 'You should be on TV more!'

Oh, and one from Danny: 'OMG! Did you just nearly swear in front of Princess Prim?! Love it!'

If only he knew.

The camera adds ten pounds

I saw myself on the big screen once. It was a truly humbling experience. A British film was going to be shooting a scene where the lead character goes to a big movie premiere in London, and the PR girls from the film company called around some of us usual red carpet reporters to see if we wanted to be in on it. I guess actors aren't as convincing as genuine journalists when it comes to looking tired, desperate and pissed-off, with a tape recorder in their hands. The film company also had an ulterior motive, I'm sure: get a few showbiz hacks into a film and they'll be so chuffed at being 'movie stars' they'll definitely want to write about the experience in their publications. It's all great press.

As a steadfast believer in 'why not', I, of course, said yes. This was back when I was still working full-time at the magazine, so my boss was overjoyed too, thinking there could be an opportunity to get some dirt on the lead actress. Thus it was that a couple of weeks later I found myself on a night shoot at a disused warehouse in the suburbs that was mocked up – pretty convincingly I have to admit – to look like an all-star West End premiere. Even in my downtime, I thought to myself bitterly, I'm standing in bloody press pens.

The shoot was frankly a bore. We shot the scene – basically me and a bunch of colleagues shouting excitedly at the red carpet arrivals – endless times, with huge gaps between each take while boys in baggy jeans and huge hooded jackets huddled around a monitor and checked each one. It was March, but meant to look like July. By the end of the night I was seriously considering going up to one of the four assistant directors and ripping the Puffa right off his back. As for the gossip on the lead actress? She was wrapped in a blanket and whisked away to her Winnebago between takes, presumably warming her million-dollar tootsies in front of a heater.

Still, I was going to be in a film – however briefly. I knew the moment would one day arrive when I'd have to go to the press screening of the finished product and watch myself. However, since films seem to take an age to be officially finished, during which time all the various editors try to shape hours of footage into something watchable, that day didn't come around quickly. In fact, it was only at a New Year's Eve party nine months later that, in a moment of pre-tequila clarity, I was recalling some of my highlights of the year and remembered that cold night's filming back in March. What had happened to it? Googling the movie's title the next day – the internet really was made for people with hangovers, wasn't it? – I discovered that my cinematic debut had at last been given a release date in spring.

After the usual round of awards ceremonies in February and March, spring finally arrived. And so, too, did an email inviting me to a 'cast and crew' screening of the film in a hotel's private screening room in Central London. To say I was nervous is the biggest understatement since Tom Cruise declared himself 'not exactly a giant'. But in the comfortable surroundings of the private cinema that night, surrounded by many of the baggy-jeaned technical crew I'd been hanging out with the year before, I soon settled down and excitedly followed the storyline in anticipation of the big premiere scene. When it finally came, I was speechless.

It wasn't just that a whole night's filming had been reduced to a mere few seconds (if it wasn't quite 'blink and you'll miss it' it was certainly 'don't nip to the toilet or it'll all be over'). More shocking, though, was seeing a scarily bloated version of me projected on to the screen. In just that tiny moment that I was in shot, I noticed a catalogue of things I considered 'wrong' with my body, all now recorded for ever, all now huge on the big screen:

Weight. Worrying about my weight has been something I've always tried to avoid, leaving it to the beauty pages of the magazines to preach about rather than getting worked up myself. Yet up there in the cinema I didn't half look chubbier than I thought I was. In my head I was Claire from Steps circa 2001. On the screen I was Claire from Steps circa 2012. The old adage about the camera adding ten pounds was scarily true.

Hair. Was it really that bright red? Why had no one told me that it just made me look really pale? And although my hair was tied back there were those awful curly wisps of hair around my temples, flyaway frizz that hadn't smoothed down properly. I would be having serious words with Henry my hairdresser.

Eye bags. Looked significantly bigger than I had expected.

Thighs. As above.

Boobs. One small mercy – at least the bra I was wearing gave me some serious uplift. Hello boys in the front row of the Odeon.

The film, of course, moved on and certainly only my closest family and friends would have even noticed me in it, let alone concerned themselves with the way that I looked. But for me it seemed to freeze frame for hours. For the rest of the film I just kept thinking about that moment in the spotlight. By the end of the week I'd joined a gym, booked a hair appointment and decluttered my wardrobe to within an inch of its life.

All of which might make you think I'm a very shallow person and it's certainly an issue that I've wrestled with myself. But here's the thing. Seeing oneself as large as that (I mean on a large screen, not just the size of my hips) is a very freaky experience, something that I think naturally forces you to question what you look like. Most of us 'normal people' only look at ourselves from one or two angles in our bedroom mirror. Seeing yourself on a cinema screen, however, is like looking into a massive version of one of those awful magnifying mirrors they have in hotel bathrooms. It's no wonder that celebrities, people whose lives are led on screen and in photos, get so paranoid about their looks. Not healthy, but understandable.

With female stars it'll be no surprise to hear that weight is the thing most panicked about. Quite why the screen seems to add weight I don't know, but it does. Which is why when I meet famous women, they're always about half the size that you think they're going to be. Like, stick thin. I've got a lot of friends who I would consider to be in good shape – but that's in the normal world. In the world of the famous, 'in good shape' means ultra-skinny and ultra-toned. Even then you're probably not satisfied. There's a very famous leading lady out there who lifts, rows and spins like a madwoman in the best gym in Beverly Hills, the result being a body that's about as curvy as a matchstick. But it's not enough. When she sits down and crosses her legs she still holds one *above* the other, rather than letting it rest, so as not to squash her thighs together and make them look 'fat'.

With guys, weight seems less of an issue. You'd be amazed how a well-cut suit can hide a beer belly and man boobs. Hair, on the other hand, is something else. Unless you're completely smooth-headed like Bruce Willis or a happy silver fox like George Clooney, going bald or grey just doesn't seem to be allowed within the high echelons of male celebrity. The boys will go to any lengths to disguise it. It's often the ones you least expect too. I know of a couple of very famous actors, guys who make a living seeming light-hearted and carefree, who are paranoid about their follicles. One insists that his groomer sprinkles those weird fibres on to his bald spot in a bid to cover up the emerging skin, while the other gets black mascara brushed into his stubble and barnet to block out the grey.

But my favourite story of a celebrity beauty routine is the male rock star who is especially particular about his mop top. Not that you'd realise if you saw him on stage or screen. His image is of the dangerous rebel, the snarling man's-man who laughs in the face of moisturiser and who wouldn't let a make-up artist even lightly dust his sweaty forehead with powder. But it's really not like that at all. Next time you see his poker-straight locks swishing along with the drum beat as he growls out another angry song just remember, he's spent hours in a salon getting his natural curls straightened with perm solution in order to look that menacing.

Not that many celebrities would admit to this (of course, I don't mean the Z-List WAGs and wannabes who'll happily sell their boob job or liposuction story to a tacky rag). Real stars keep schtum about all the hard work, because, as a larger than life icon, it's meant to all look effortless and natural. That's why they're called stars – they're supposedly untouchable and out of reach to us mere mortals. Only those for whom stardom is not the be all and end all seem confident enough to admit that, actually, their glamour is all an illusion. Cate Blanchett, one of the finest actresses around, who always seems to look genuinely stunning as opposed to desperately over-preened, once said that as soon as she gets back from a premiere she's out of the outfit a stylist chose for her, stripped of the make-up a professional lovingly applied, and is slobbing out in her PJs, barefaced and mopping up baby sick before you can say 'after party'. *That's* reality. For so many in the celebrity world, however, reality isn't something that they want to admit to. You want to try to push it to one side. Having seen 'the real' lumpy me on the big screen, I can understand why.

Food

It always makes me laugh when I watch a Hollywood movie and there's some joke in there about awful health food or crazy alternative diets. The actors in the movie might be desperately trying to appear normal and down-to-earth, as cynical about supposed super foods as the average person on the street, but in reality they're the worst offenders. Hollywood is the home of the picky eater, no matter how many times an actress can claim in interviews that she likes to scoff her face with cakes just like everyone else. Back in the day it was illegal narcotics that so many celebs were hooked on. Now the drugs of choice are way more legal if still dubious – akai berry, maple syrup, protein-only. Fad diets rule.

A source once told me about an incident with a famous leading lady who, frankly, just didn't eat. Her actor boyfriend of the time was a lot less of a head case and one night at an industry dinner he'd had enough. In between the necessary schmoozing of producers and directors, he gallantly tried to get his squeeze to actually get some nosh inside of her. Easier said than done. Those sitting at the same table were treated to the sight of this leading lady essentially being spoon-fed like a baby by her hunky other half, whining at him and straining her head away from the morsels of food on the end of his fork. After much effort on his part he finally gave in. The actress had managed the princely sum of half an artichoke and quarter of a tomato. They split up a few weeks later.

Why did she behave like that? Like I've said, if you have the spotlight shining so brightly on you paranoia can quickly set in. What can start out as a sensible desire to be healthy quickly morphs into an obsession about weight and looks. It's the reason why one pop star lady was reported to have shunned any food during a long photo shoot, deciding instead to merely suck the juice from a pile of strawberries (even though she was already thin as a rake).

Then there's the very famous TV and movie actor, well known for his laddish persona and cheeky roles, who's so obsessed with his health that he pays several hundred pounds a day to get all his meals delivered to him by a nutritionist who controls his diet using strict macrobiotic principles. In my experience, it's often the ones that you least expect. Watch this guy in a movie and he acts like he's only interested in burgers and fries.

I suppose on the flip side, some stars are the complete opposite, wearing their puritanical diets proudly and making a name for themselves as not only actors but icons of healthy living. They don't want to hide what's in their fridge. It's not always how it seems, though. One star we all know is famed for such a lifestyle – has even made a bit of a secondary career out of it. What might surprise you is that her actual diet isn't half as perfect as she likes to claim it is. In public she might waffle on about gluten-free and vegan recipes but in private she'll knock back a bloody steak like she's a famished rugby player. The message? Never judge a book by its cover. For some performers, everything in life is just a big act.

Stars' eating habits are one thing when they're confined to their own home, but when they're out on tour or doing press it's down to the poor publicists and assistants to make sure their client's every whim is catered for. I pity the poor minion who had to source freshly squeezed carrot juice for one movie star when he was out in the middle of nowhere on a shoot. A bottle from the local supermarket just wouldn't be good enough. After calling up the hotel where he was staying (several miles from the film set) to check they had a juicer and plenty of veg, then booking a car to transport the drink, a couple of hours later four bottles of the orange nectar turned up in the star's Winnebago. Surely the first bottles of juice to have their own chauffeur?

My own experience of a star's diet was a lot less glamorous, though. There I was trying to interview a bulky comedy star and coax some vaguely coherent answers out of him – but he had other ideas. In the middle of the interview a huge spread of food arrived on a room-service trolley and the big fella decided that he wanted to chow down right that instant. I carried my recording equipment over from the sofa to the table where he now sat and tried to carry on the same thread of conversation. To his credit, he kept on speaking even as he shovelled spoonfuls of Chinese chicken and potato salad into his gob. It's just that, with his mouth stuffed, what he was saying was barely coherent. Could he have waited to fill his belly? Of course. But food is a surprisingly complex accessory among the rich and famous, used to show off the huge chasm between 'us' and 'them'. Just like the A-Listers who like to brag about their own flawless diets, this guy wanted to show me who was boss. He could do whatever the hell he wanted and scoffing his plentiful lunch on my time was just one of them. Back in the office that afternoon, tucking into my packet of crisps and homemade cheese sarnie as I worked away on the computer, I'd never felt smaller. Even worse, my thighs felt huge.

Beauty

I was once asked to write an article on how much it costs celebrities to keep looking so damn good. For anyone who thought they can get by on a pot of Olay and a prayer, think again. The figures go something like this:

Botox on the forehead (every 3 months): £300
Fillers in frown lines and around the mouth (every 6 months): £600
  (2 syringes)
Hair coloured and cut (every 6 weeks): £200
Spray tan (every fortnight): £50
Manicure and pedicure (every 6 weeks): £75
Facial (every week): £100
Massage (every week): £100
Personal trainer (3 times a week): £225
Nutritionist/chef: £1,000 per week
Stylist: £750 per event
Hair and make-up artist: £800 per event
Teeth whitening (3 times a year): £3,000

All of which adds up to an eye-watering annual expenditure well into six figures (and that's assuming that our star gets most of their clothes and daily beauty products given to them for free, with brands being so desperate to associate with the glitterati). Sounds a lot, right? Luckily the celebrities' faces are normally so full of Botox they can't look surprised by the bill. It all just goes to show, though: that 'effortlessly beautiful' actress you read about in the glossies every week actually needs a hell of a lot of work to appear so casually stunning.

After the piece came out, my editor at the time was impressed enough to ask me to try out some of the quirkiest products currently wowing showbiz royalty with their miraculous effects. I didn't have to be asked twice. After contacting a plethora of beauty PR teams, eventually parcels started arriving through my postbox, producing extreme amounts of brazen jealousy from my flatmate. If I thought a moisturiser with caviar in it (costing a cool £200 a jar) was strange enough it was nothing compared to the pot of Pure Snail Serum Lotion (containing '100% Helix Aspersa Müller Snail extract' – great for blemishes, apparently). 'Katie Holmes supposedly swears by it,' I told myself as I gingerly patted it on to my cheeks that night, Erica looking on in horror as if I had finally lost my mind. By the time I was sent information on a 'gold leaf and sheep placenta' facial that'd been linked to Victoria Beckham I felt less like a showbiz journalist, more like a witch.

So did these fantastical products actually work, you ask? Well, yes. If I looked closely I could see that all the things that were meant to happen, did happen: fresher-looking skin, a peachier complexion, etc. Unfortunately, when the lotions and potions ran low so did my youthful glow – and I wasn't going to be shelling out hundreds of quid for more, miracle ingredients or no miracle ingredients. So I went back to basics. To be honest, no one except me really noticed the difference.

The truth is, the beauty business is as full of gimmicks as the showbiz world itself. What's the latest trend? What's the new buzz word? Who's getting all the press? That's not to say that some things don't deserve the hype, whether they're a hot rejuvenating serum or a cool new singer, but it's healthier not to get too swept along by the headlines. Just because something's the new favourite doesn't mean its effects will last.

After a few weeks of high-level primping and preening, I had just one treatment left to try: laser hair removal. A girl representing the company whispered to me in confidence that a well-known glamour model has her underarms done, so I thought that if it's good enough for someone who spends most of her life semi-naked, I'd best give it a go. God knows I'd spent enough time keeping everything pristine over the years, since men seem to morph into outraged grooming experts at even the slightest hint of hair growth on a woman's body, as if we're suddenly something from *Planet of the Apes*.

As I had a beach holiday looming I decided to do my bikini line. A few sessions of this treatment, I was informed as I booked my appointment, and I could wave goodbye to the razor for ever. Hair follicles apparently don't recover after being zapped by a ray gun.

At the salon (discreetly located on the top floor of an exclusive department store), I was met by Brigit, a smiley beautician clad in a white coat and with meticulous make-up. She looked to me as if she wouldn't hurt a fly. I was wrong. After being shown into the treatment room I stripped down to my bra and pants and she applied some ice cold clear gel on to my target areas. Bit odd, I thought, but whatever . . . The fact that my eyes had to be protected by wraparound shades probably should have told me everything I needed to know, but still nothing could have prepared me for the sensation when beaming Brigit got going with her electromagnetic radiation. I can only describe the sensation as like someone flicking a scorching hot elastic band around my crotch. I admit that I've thankfully never had someone *really* flicking a scorching hot elastic band around my crotch, so perhaps the two feelings are completely different, but I've got a pretty good idea I'm on the right track. Channelling my old school PE teacher, I repeated the phrase 'No pain, no gain' over and over in my head, like some New Age mantra. Finally, the whir of the machine died down and my legs relaxed again. Relief. Unfortunately before I had even properly regained my wherewithal, still blissfully in a post-laser daze, I found myself agreeing to follow up this complimentary session with a bunch of more costly appointments 'to really penetrate the hair matrix' (as Brigit poetically put it). I left the room with a head full of holiday daydreams . . . and a walk like Liam Gallagher.

My article ended with three simple words of advice to anyone heading to a salon in search of similarly hairless celebrity skin: 'Don't Forget Painkillers.'

Clash of the egos

You can't get on with everyone, and I couldn't get on with Nicola. Back in my days as a staff writer, Nicola from Accounts was my office nemesis. Nicola and I met on my first day in my first job, when I had to sort out my payment details with her. *Not* a good start. While Nicola looked like the sort of person who had a file for all her supermarket receipts, just so she could monitor the fluctuating prices of cat food and baked beans, I was about as financially savvy as a Greek banker. I still am, to be honest. Just walking over to her austere part of the office, the only picture on her notice board a cutting from the *Daily Mail* with the headline 'Rip-off Britain!', sent shivers down my spine. Fumbling with my bank details and having to ask her what 'PAYE' was, she quickly took a dislike to my less ordered approach to money matters. Things only got worse. She considered my frequent inability to hand in expense claims on time and loud giggling sessions with my colleagues to be crimes worthy of prison time. I never knew that the sound of someone tutting could be so loud.

A possible thawing of hostilities occurred when she once asked me, gingerly and out of the blue, if there were any preview tickets going for the movie version of *Mamma Mia!* 'I've seen it on the stage four times,' she quietly admitted, fiddling with the buttons of her mauve blouse. Suddenly this stocky, starkly dressed middle-aged woman seemed vaguely human to me, for the first time. Unfortunately the next week I headed off on holiday for a fortnight and only remembered about her ticket request when I was sunbathing by the pool in Ibiza and 'Dancing Queen' popped up randomly on my iPod. By the time I got back to work, the film was already out. Apologising to Nicola for being so forgetful on my first day back, she simply smiled condescendingly, looked me up and down, then announced: 'You know a suntan is just dead skin don't you?' Nicola sure knew how to kill a conversation. So when I explained to you earlier that I went freelance in order to be my own boss, I forgot to mention that there was also another reason: I did it to escape working in close proximity with women like Nicola.

Still, very few people are lucky enough to work only with people that they like, and it's no different for celebrities. At some point even the biggest star in the world will probably have to associate with their own version of Nicola from Accounts. 'The camera never lies', so the old saying goes. Unfortunately, that is just one big porky. Next time you look at a movie poster or an album cover where the stars are all beaming happily back at you, don't be fooled by the body language. Just as you and I don't get on with everyone we work with – it's naïve of us to think that famous people are all bosom buddies too. So much of acting is, after all, about faking friendships with relative strangers for the purposes of entertainment.

So how do actors cope if they don't actually get on with their co-stars? Simple. The making of a movie doesn't last for ever (unlike some office jobs) – if any grievances crop up on-set, they know that they'll usually be over as soon as the filming is done and everyone has moved on to other projects. Chalk it up to a few months' experience. The end.

Until the movie comes out, is a huge success and – horror of horrors – sequels are requested. Stars who hoped they'd seen the back of each other realise painfully that their next few years (and next few pay packets) are tied up in them looking like BFFs. Sure, they don't have to say yes but a big cheque being waved in front of you can be a very persuasive thing. So, forget Daniel Day-Lewis method acting – it's those thespians who hate each other's guts but have to pretend otherwise that really deserve the acting awards.

Take the lead actors of one particularly popular movie franchise. These two action heroes have acted like best buddies endlessly over the last few years, but the reality is something very different. Each star thinks that he's the main draw of the series and neither wants to be seen as playing second fiddle to the other. Such ego games make life difficult for the publicity team when they're organising premieres for the boys, especially when it comes to the question of who arrives at the cinema last (and is therefore seen as the 'headliner' and bigger name). The carefully contrived solution? These two precious personalities have to turn up at exactly the same time, get equal billing from the announcer ('Ladies and gentlemen, Mr X and Mr Y – Mr Y and Mr X') and run on to the stage from opposite sides, meeting in the middle. When it comes to trying to keep everyone happy, the Middle East peace process has got nothing on negotiating with these two. You often see these kinds of power games on film posters too. The star whose name is on the left is traditionally the bigger, but sometimes the next one along can be placed slightly higher, to counteract the fact they're second in line. There's the question of whose face is in the foreground and whose is more in the background too. Check out the careful positioning of Bruce Willis, Channing Tatum and Dwayne Johnson (aka The Rock) in the poster for that recent awful GI Joe movie for a great example of this. It probably took months of meetings to get to a stage where everyone was happy.

The average person on the street probably never even notices the subtleties of billings, but to the star's agent, the endless emails and late-night calls to hammer out such a deal make them feel worthwhile.

Maybe it's a boy thing, the Hollywood equivalent of lads comparing themselves in the gym shower to see who's the best endowed? I've heard of another big male name from a movie franchise who is so paranoid about his co-star getting better treatment than him, he gets his minions to measure the hotel rooms that they stay in on promotional tours. God help the room booker if his on-screen rival gets a suite with more square footage than him.

Certainly the ladies who can't stand each other's company seem to keep things a lot simpler. Those glamorous girl band mates that you've heard don't get on? It's probably true. But forget the complex power games and one-upmanship. These lasses just refuse to be in a room together unless the cameras are on. Old-fashioned loathing makes things so much easier.

Stars, obviously, rarely want their feuds to become public knowledge, but some are so strongly rumoured they're almost common knowledge: Danni Minogue and Sharon Osbourne during their time as rival judges on *The X Factor*; Lily Allen and Cheryl Cole, after the Girls Aloud singer called Lily, rather unkindly, 'a chick with a dick'; Elton John and Madonna, not helped when Madge beat Sir Elt in the 'Best Original Song' category at the Golden Globes a few years back. That said, there aren't that many stars that Elton *hasn't* had a spat with.

On a more positive note, there are still plenty of stories of the most unlikely of A-List friendships, chalk-and-cheese stars finding they have more in common than anyone expected. Who would have known that Colin Farrell was great friends with the late Elizabeth Taylor, a woman well over twice his age? He even gave a reading at her funeral in 2011. Or that Vin Diesel would go backstage at a London theatre one night to personally ask Dame Judi Dench to be in a movie with him since he was such a fan (thus *The Chronicles of Riddick* was born)? If a bruiser and a Dame can find a common bond, then maybe there's hope yet for Nicola and me?

Money

Part I: Big Bucks

Money seems to be everywhere in the showbiz world. Apart from in the bank accounts of journalists, that is; I realised a long time ago that if you want to get rich, my line of work isn't the way to do it. Being an entertainment reporter is all about marvelling at how rich *other people* are.

It all comes down to publicity. I've been flown First Class all around the world, from Moscow to Marrakech, by film and record companies entirely beholden to the power of press coverage. Why? They all know that getting an audience aware of a new product is half the battle; no one's going to go and see a film or buy a song if they don't know that it's even out. That's where I come in. What better way to make sure I plug their product in a mag or online than by wooing me with a luxury trip?

I know what you're thinking: isn't that just bribery? I try to see it more as a well-oiled machine, a long established bit of mutual backscratching. For my part, I give readers some insight (hopefully) into their favourite stars by getting some great access. For the money men, I'm one of the many journalists helping to spread their word. It's only common sense that they might want to treat us well; an album launch with dodgy catering or a film junket in a ropey hotel might be all it takes for a journalist to not want to champion their product. That's not a risk any producer wants to take. In other words, it's all a process. If that process costs a massive corporation a bit of cash, then so be it. When their film strikes big at the box office or their album sells millions then any outlay is more than recouped. So I get to meet some famous people in an exotic location, have a little chat, and then a few million dollars later some mogul gets to buy a new yacht with his profits. Maybe not entirely fair, but I'm not complaining. (It doesn't work all the time, of course. It seems that no amount of press, marketing and advertising could convince people to buy Tulisa's album.)

I learnt about this big-spending very early on, when a colleague told me how he'd just returned from touring with a well-known DJ around America. It was a gruelling experience; only when you're forced to haul your arse from one side of the States to another do you appreciate just how vast a country it is. Still, the dance music star was now starting to make inroads and his record company was watching the cash flood in from gig bookings and MTV airplay. So why wouldn't they say yes to another ten grand on the budget, just to cover the star's drugs habit? A Top 10 album in the USA and suddenly that few thousand is forgotten quicker than Mr Turntable can snort up a line of Colombia's finest. When it works, showbiz offers the kind of interest rate that us lot can only dream of.

It's weird, then, that sometimes the mega-wealthy seem to be stingier than anyone else. I'm talking about the stars here, not the suits. I suppose that when you get used to everything being paid for you, company flunkies flitting around you like giant wallet-wasps, having to put your hand in your *own* pocket hurts even more.

Take the loaded fashion designer who'd had a big party at one of the swankiest hotels in Mayfair. The morning after, just before checking out, she remembered that she and her posh pals had been raiding the mini-bar in her room all night and that the tiny fridge was now virtually empty. Unwilling to pay the hotel's over-the-odds prices for a packet of cashews and a can of vodka and tonic, she sent her flunkies out to the local Tesco to pick up identical stock at supermarket prices. Five minutes of hasty rearranging later and it's like she'd never had that alcohol-fuelled craving for Pringles at 3 a.m.

Then there was the movie star who was on an international tour promoting a film that had his name above the title. Trying to look glamorous after arriving at his hotel, he tipped the bellboy for carrying his bags. When an assistant explained the exchange rate and the actor worked out just how much he'd handed over, his frugal ways kicked in. Cue an awkward moment with an A-List movie star demanding that a lowly hotel porter gives him change. (What is it about loaded people tipping? I've even heard of an Oscar winner who likes to give three-figure tips to hotel staff when he's signing for room service. Sounds generous, until you realise he only does it when he knows a film company are footing his bills. The result? It gets out to the press that this guy's a saint for being so giving, while a red-faced PR girl has to explain to her studio boss why this fella's breakfast in bed cost £500.)

Part II: Tight Wads

Not all huge entertainment companies splash the cash, though. There's one corporation that's notoriously tight. And, so it should be, since it's actually *our* pennies that keep it going. Yes, I'm talking about the dear old BBC. It's known around the world for its impartial journalism, groundbreaking drama and cherished comedy, but don't ever think it throws around money like a drunken Lottery winner. I've not only experienced the occasional tiny freelance payments from 'Auntie', paid out with all the relish of a Middle East dictator handing over power, I've also 'enjoyed' their hospitality . . .

It had been one week since I returned from an all-expenses-paid trip to LA where I was pampered at the expense of a major film company. I now found myself in a basement room at the Beeb's old TV Centre in Shepherd's Bush. It might be the one-time location of childhood favourites such as *Top of the Pops*, *Blue Peter* and *Newsround*, but its maze-like corridors are more reminiscent of a high-security prison than a glamorous home-to-the-stars. I'm seated – in one of those grey plastic ones with a hole on the back like you had at school – in the junket room, squinting as the strip lighting beams down from overhead. I half-smile at the dozen other miserable-looking reporters in the room, before a harassed-looking BBC press officer finally comes in with the *EastEnders* stars we are about to interview. I put aside the notes I've been making, hoping that no one from the corporation spots what I've written:

HOLLYWOOD	BBC
Veuve Clicquot	Happy Shopper orange juice
Blinis and caviar	Twiglets and crisps
A banqueting table	A hostess trolley
Angelina Jolie	Barbara Windsor

Luckily Babs is a joy to talk to, but as she talks about playing Peggy Mitchell, sipping her water from a plastic cup and still wearing her coat thanks to the lack of heating in the room, California seems like a long way away.

So if you've ever worried that our licence fee is being squandered let me reassure you with two words: *I wish*.

Kate Moss

Being a showbiz reporter has got me into some amazing parties. Before I arrived in London I'd never even tasted champagne. Now I actually have a *favourite brand*. While the left-wing student in me feels guilty for falling for the ridiculous showiness of it all, sometimes you just have to give credit where credit's due. Swigging Moët from a crystal flute as you stand on a million-dollar yacht overlooking the harbour at Cannes is a breathtaking experience, socialist or not. That said, such an experience does have the unique ability to somehow make you feel both incredibly special and utterly inadequate at the same time. When I leave a flashy party I don't, unlike the hosts, head back in a limo to my penthouse or mansion. I usually get the night bus to the nearest stop to my flat then walk the rest, cursing my heels all the way.

Sometimes, though, *not* letting on that you're a journalist gets you into better places than any press card could. That's how, one night, I found myself partying with Kate Moss. First of all, albeit begrudgingly, I should at least partly thank an ex for the experience. It wasn't a long relationship, but it did coincide with a time when he was friends, through work, with a guy who was part of Kate's circle – six degrees of separation and all that. When this friend decided to throw himself a party for a big birthday, my ex found himself on the invite list alongside the world's most famous supermodel. And I was his plus one. 'Sod the painful walk home,' I thought to myself as I got ready that night. 'Hanging with Kate is going to need the most killer heels I can find.'

I'd been fascinated with Ms Moss for a long time. This is partly because I never failed to like her tastes; I'd copy her style like a young girl looking up to her older sister. In her early days as an indie waif I tried to mimic her by living in Kurt Cobain-style checked shirts and dousing myself in CK One. During her time as a Camden rock 'n' roller alongside Pete Doherty, meanwhile, I was living near the area and therefore deemed myself rebellious-by-association. In reality I spent less time caning it, more time slobbing out on the sofa and watching re-runs of *Friends*, but the sentiment was there. I am just one of thousands of girls who has followed Kate's every metamorphosis with admiration, fascination and a desperation to look as good in jean shorts as she does.

Kate Moss is also intriguing to millions, like me, for one very simple reason: she never lets us believe that she's anything else. Generally refusing to talk to the press, we know her primarily from pouty photos and achingly hip outfits. She's never allowed herself the chance to ruin her image by opening her gob and saying something stupid. A clever move. She's a great example of creating a mystique around oneself. The less we know, the more we want to know. It's no surprise that her motto is apparently 'never complain, never explain'.

All of which makes me certain that if she'd known there was a showbiz journalist at the party with her – trying not to stare but probably doing a very bad job of it – she wouldn't have been happy. Kate has a tight group of friends, all of whom she trusts not to expose her. The party-giver was obviously one of them. But there I was, a shameless fan and worse – a reporter – desperate to catch a glimpse of the regular person underneath the edgy façade. While I was never going to write anything about the party in the magazine, enjoying my weekend being 'off the clock', by now I had a built-in journalist's curiosity that wouldn't have been welcomed had people known about my job.

I can't help but gawp though. Who wouldn't, right? Looking incredible in tight black leather trousers, Kate smiled, giggled and skipped her way around the party, busting a few dodgy moves on the dancefloor and flirting with an eighties teen pop star along the way. I couldn't believe it. The attitude that comes out for every pap and hack was nowhere to be seen. Here was just a girl – and she was way more 'girly' than I expected – letting her (completely fabulous) hair down. The two-dimensional figure I was so used to seeing snaps of in my magazines had grown into a real three-dimensional human being, someone much more friendly, fun and 'normal' than I'd ever imagined. Albeit with a significantly better bum than most of us.

I headed back home that night dreaming of this easier way of hanging out with the beautiful people, one where I don't have to do an interview or hunt down some gossip just to justify my presence. A few weeks later, though, my then boyfriend kindly decided that 'he just wasn't looking for commitment right now' and my brief link to The Court of Kate was severed. But every time I see a roadside billboard or magazine ad with her on it, pouting and looking effortlessly chic, I still remember us standing next to each other on the dancefloor and jumping about like idiots to some old Ska tune. I'd been a fan for so long I felt that I knew her like a relative. Luckily for me she had absolutely no idea who I was.

Cannes

Whole books could be written about the craziness of the Cannes Film Festival. To those who've never been, the stock images that come to mind are usually those of starlets posing for photo shoots on the Croisette (the town's long stretch of seafront) and of glitzy premieres for highly anticipated new films. Both of these pictures are true. But the craziness . . . that's something you can only really understand by being there.

The harsh truth is, I don't go to the Cannes Film Festival to watch films. There's far too much other stuff to report on. While I have braved some 8.30 a.m. screenings of newsworthy movies, queuing for an hour alongside the thousands of other tired and hungover journalists, each of us with our all-important, colour-coded festival pass around our neck, it's not something I do often. That's for the film critics with nothing else to do all day but watch stuff (a luxury I've often found myself dreaming of).

No, as a reporter I mostly find myself running from swanky hotel to swanky hotel, often at opposite ends of the town, trying to get to press conferences, film launches and interviews on time. Smaller festivals might try to schedule these so that they don't clash with one another. Cannes, unfortunately, is just too sprawling to be bespoke. It's for this reason that my main bit of advice to

163

anyone heading to the Côte d'Azur for their first festival is always: wear comfy shoes.

Here's a typical day at Cannes:

7 a.m. Get up, wash and dress.

8 a.m. Black coffee and croissant.

8.15 a.m. Another black coffee and another croissant. It's going to be a long day.

8 a.m. Call work and give them a rundown of what I'm expecting the day to hold (with the caveat that this is Cannes and therefore likely to *entirely* change).

9 a.m. Leave the hotel and begin the long walk into town.

Cannes is a deceptively big place, a seaside resort with suburbs that seem to go on for miles. If you want to stay near the centre during the festival then you'll be shelling out some serious euros for the privilege. Hence why most journalists stay a little way out in order to walk in and save money (with the bonus of seriously improved calf muscles after a fortnight of all that striding).

10 a.m. Attend press launch for a new film. Invites are hard to come by, but if you chase hard enough, the PR teams looking after the event can normally be worn down. These kind of launches usually involve seeing a few clips of the film then hearing a bit from the cast and crew, all of whom have been flown into France to drum up interest in the movie. Drumming is what I love. It means I'll be able to grab a few words with a couple of the stars and get it online by lunchtime.

I'll be honest: with these events taking place on hotel roofs and private beaches, and, of course, in the golden sunshine that's so common in the south of France in the early summer, it's impossible not to be swayed by the radiant glamour of it all. It's remarkable how quickly aching feet and sweaty armpits become insignificant when you're sat chatting to a gorgeous movie star with the sunshine beating down on you. But that's really the danger of Cannes – it's all smoke and mirrors. For example, I once interviewed a talentless glamour girl just a few feet away from the clear lapping waters of the Mediterranean, convinced as the 80-degree heat warmed my shoulders that her new film would be a chic masterpiece. When I actually saw it back in rainy London it was a piece of crap. Much like the hypnotic power of a holiday romance, the sun-kissed continental allure of Cannes can make even us hardened journos believe that something pitiful could actually be a big deal. It's why so many film companies want to launch their products there. Hordes of pasty hacks who rarely see daylight can't believe they've actually been allowed to leave the office and head to the coast. They're so drunk on sunshine (and French rosé) that they'll say *anything* looks good.

11 a.m. Head to the Palais – a huge complex by the beach that's the hub of the festival, housing umpteen cinemas, cafés and conference rooms – to use the free WiFi. There's no time to waste uploading the quick chat I've just had.

12 p.m. Une baguette au jambon et un Perrier.

12.30 p.m. There's another press event happening down the other end of the Croisette. On a clear day I could walk there in ten minutes, but with Cannes' seafront packed like Oxford Street on Christmas Eve for the entire 11 days of the festival, I need to allow extra time to barge sauntering French people out of the way.

1 p.m. A press event for a major new Hollywood animation, featuring the voices of some of the biggest stars in the world. We're promised 'something special'. In other words, some high-concept gimmick designed to get the snappers' shutters going like crazy. It's these pictures that get seen around the world and can give a film a huge promotional push. When you're there on the ground though, the bigger the event just means the bigger the bun fight.

That's not to say that some of these stunts during the festival haven't been highly entertaining, even if the films they've been promoting haven't been. Some of my favourites that I've witnessed include:

1. Will Smith, Angelina Jolie and Jack Black being dragged around the Med on a banana boat, to publicise the (not very good) film *Shark Tale*.

2. A variety of young British actresses prancing around the seafront in school uniforms to publicise the (not very good) St Trinian's movie.

3. Jean-Claude Van Damme arriving at a party by speed boat, to publicise a film that I can't even remember (but probably wasn't very good).

4. And of course Sacha Baron Cohen, as Borat, debuting his lime green mankini on the beach, as a nod to Cannes legend Brigitte Bardot. *That* film was actually great to watch – unlike Sacha's disturbingly exposed butt cheeks.

The point being, once you get away from the arty directors entering their films into the festival's super serious competition,

Cannes is really just style over substance. It's a circus, with the world's entertainment industry all happily soaking up the beauty of the surroundings, blissfully unaware that really they're just clowns. I've been to press launches of films that never actually get made, the festival just used to publicise an *idea*. I've been to parties in Cannes promoting jewellery companies where a top pop star is paid thousands to perform for a few minutes, before being flown back home. What's that got to do with films? I've even necked rosé with balloon-breasted porn stars on a yacht, rented for a fortnight by the world's biggest adult entertainment company. Talk about shallow.

Purists, of course, don't like the fact that what was once a chin-stroking celebration of quality international film-making has now been hijacked by these slick chancers wanting to harness the holiday atmosphere and get some instant publicity for their products. Showbiz journos like me, on the other hand, are less harsh. I know Cannes is full of silly stunts and shameless hype but, on the other hand, I'm relieved that it never fails to give me something to write about.

3 p.m. The launch is over – and the press conference that followed safely recorded and ready to transcribe – so I head back along the Croisette, stopping only to reapply some Factor 50 to my nose. Along the front the restaurants are packed with movie types having drinks, while the pavement is bursting with endless buskers, sightseers and North African men trying to sell knock-off sunglasses. All I want to do is run down to the beach and jump in the sea. Unfortunately, in Cannes, the welcoming Med is strictly look-but-don't-touch. There just isn't the time.

3.30 p.m. I drop in on several hotels on my walk back, each housing film and PR companies' temporary offices for the duration of the festival. I need to stay in touch with these people every day, to keep on their radar should a major celeb decide to pay a visit out of the blue and they're the ones looking after them. As every other reporter in the world seems to be doing the same thing – 'Hello, I'm Anders from *Spløt!* magazine in Denmark and I'm wanting to interview Uma Thurman' – I have to queue for quite a while. It's a good job I do since I end up getting invited to a beauty event tomorrow that's promising Eva Longoria. You see what I mean about Cannes not being about films any more? I'm just as likely to be speaking to someone about moisturiser.

4.30 p.m. Back in my hotel room, shoes off and feet up, writing up the afternoon's events.

6.30 p.m. After a day of rushing around the town, evenings offer only a brief respite for food before the parties begin. Huge phone bills are run up trying to persuade publicists that you should be on the guest list for their bash and that you'll definitely mention it in your next article. The problem is, with Cannes being a town basically full of gossiping journalists for those 11 days, whatever party you're at you soon hear on the grapevine that the one down the road is even better. Your party might have Dannii Minogue in the VIP area but you can bet your life that the one you're *not* at has Kylie in theirs. Cue more expensive, begging phone calls to stressed PR girls.

10 p.m. The parties at Cannes are rarely a let-down on the glamour front. I've stared at everything from ice sculptures to fire breathers as I've nibbled on mini spring rolls and salmon fishcakes. They also offer the chance for some unlikely sights and new stories. That Oscar-winning actor who couldn't get into a party one year, and who decided to give the doormen the whole 'Do you know who I am?' routine, probably should have thought twice before he blew his top in front of so many of us journalists.

Still, parties are only as good as the people at them. A bash costing thousands still means nothing if you don't know anyone that's there. So after a few hours at these parties, I've been known to jump into a cab and head up to the iconic Hôtel du Cap, set a few miles up the coast in Antibes. It's in this luxurious, castle-style mansion that many A-Listers stay during their time at the festival and, if you've got deep enough pockets, you can have a drink in the bar and watch the glitterati of the entertainment world let their hair down around you. As it's a hotel that only takes cash and the drinks are *really* expensive, you need to be prepared though. What's more, look too much like a snooping journalist and the maître d' will have you out on your ear quicker than you can say *Un tap water s'il vous plaît*. Many's the time I've had to casually pay three-figure drinks bills as if it meant nothing to me, trying not to look too pauper-like and silently praying that my boss back in Blighty would be feeling generous when I file my expenses claim. Get some gossip on Jen or J-Lo, though, and it's usually worth it.

1 a.m. Then in the small hours, as the movie stars head to their massive suites, I jump back into a taxi and head to my tiny hotel room on the outskirts of town to collate everything I've got that day. In Cannes, even a quiet day usually means that you have plenty of content. With a sunburnt nose, sore feet and severely depleted purse I nearly always sleep soundly, collapsing into the bed after an 18-hour day. Like I said, it's a crazy place. In a few hours' time it's back on with the trainers and the SPF, ready to jump on to the treadmill all over again. The Cannes Film Festival – the world's most glamorous assembly line.

Secrets

Thankfully, a lot has changed over the last few decades. Generally speaking, in the UK at least, people no longer have to hide who they really are. In most areas of the showbiz world we're so used to gay celebrities – from mouthy TV presenters to respected elder thespians to pretty teen pop stars – that no one really even bats an eyelid if someone comes out (even 'coming out' seems antiquated in an era where it's normally so blatantly obvious for what side someone's batting, they don't even have to make an announcement any more). The fact is, I'm probably more surprised when someone in the media turns out *not* to be gay.

However, there's still one area of entertainment where being 'out' remains, shamefully, a big no-no: Hollywood.

Being gay isn't, in itself, what fascinates us journalists. I've been poetically described as a 'fag hag' enough times to be totally blasé about what my gay mates get up to. No, it's the *keeping it secret* that's the intriguing part. And there's no place quite so full of secrets as the Hollywood film industry. Well-known theatre and TV names such as John Barrowman, Neil Patrick Harris and Rupert Everett might all have made their sexuality clear to the world, but when it comes to leading men in huge movies there's still a conspicuous silence.

So what is it that these in-the-closet movie stars think they would lose if they were honest? The answer, like so many things in Hollywood, is, of course, money. Producers – for the most part – still can't handle an openly gay man playing a straight leading role, especially if it is a traditional tough guy kind of character. They're petrified that audiences will be put off by such trickery, so the stars worry that their fat paycheques will stop rolling in.

But isn't that what acting is all about? Pretending? Daniel Craig's not really a spy, Meryl Streep doesn't really walk around singing Abba and Robert Downey Jr's not an actual superhero. Surely we have enough imagination to buy into a great performance, whatever the star gets up to in their bedroom? For some stars, though, that pretence of movie acting spills over into their personal life too. They're playing a straight character on the big screen and they continue to play a straight character for the press and fans – even if their publicists might know different.

I truly believe that we've got the tolerance to cope with a movie icon being gay. All we need is for someone to be brave enough to be the first and kickstart the process. Of course, you might argue that coming out shouldn't be forced on celebs and it's certainly true that many stars are happy to keep their private lives just that, private, regardless of whether they've got anything to 'hide'. Fair enough. But those men who pretend to the press that they're dating a certain female – as a way to gain column inches – should surely show some courage. The irony is, the most high-profile, secretly gay A-Listers are all known for their action man roles. On screen, they're heroes. But they're still too chicken to be true to themselves.

Movie stars are icons like few others. Just think of the influence they could have if they were living examples of honesty and tolerance. While the sports world also needs to 'man up' about an issue largely swept under the carpet, it seems extra silly to me that what is supposedly such a creative and liberal environment (unlike, say, football or rugby) can't actually practise what it preaches. Acting is an amazing thing and on the big screen it's simply magical. But is there really any need to keep up an act when the cameras have stopped rolling?

Rihanna

As someone fascinated by fame and achievement, I always presume that hugely successful stars are older than me simply because of what they've accomplished. In my thirty-something years I've got to be a moderately successful journalist with a moderately decent income and moderately nice flat. Anyone who's achieved more than that kind of moderation has to be older than I am, right? After all, it was the senior kids in school who were so far ahead of you, so shouldn't it be the same in life?

Unfortunately, the older I get the more I realise that this is painfully far from true. I can be in awe of Gaga's creativity and Blake Lively's wardrobe all I want (and I am quite a lot) but when you do the math, it's pretty clear that while I'm not quite long enough in the tooth to be their actual mother, I could easily be their significantly older sister. When I was their age, I was barely out of college. They, on the other hand, are millionaires. Many stars might *seem* world-weary because of the things that they've experienced, the influence they wield and because their pictures are constantly plastered in every magazine, newspaper and gossip site, but in reality, lots of them are just incredibly young.

The most extreme example of this that I've encountered is Rihanna. As someone who's been in the charts – and the news – pretty much constantly for the last five years, I find it extra hard to think of her as only being born in 1988. In the last year alone she apparently earned around $53 million, yet at the time of writing she's still only 25. Her songs, videos and album covers are all so familiar, it's as if she's a wise old-timer who's been around for ever. She's now even released her own clothing line. So when I met her I was understandably surprised to find someone who's just . . . a girl.

That's not to say she wasn't impressive . . .

Taller than I imagined and – annoyingly – more beautiful and feminine than her often hard image would lead you to believe, this one-name icon, known to her family as Robyn Fenty, is ridiculously upbeat and friendly. She isn't even late for the interview, as rumours of her diva-like behaviour have often led us to believe to be a trait of hers. I must admit, the '7 countries, 7 gigs, 7 days' tour that she undertook to promote her album *Unapologetic* (you guessed it, her 7th) sounded horrendous, with tales of Ri Ri's tardiness and moods quickly hitting the web as fuming bloggers stuck on her chartered jet vented their anger on Twitter and Facebook. But the woman I meet, a few months before that, is actually *early*.

If her charm and time-keeping surprise me, they're nothing compared to the shock of just how young she is. Here's someone whom money men rely on to produce albums that generate millions, keeping a company afloat, but when it comes down to it she's still just a young girl who likes to have a good time. Her Bajan accent remains strong (it's easy to forget that she's not actually American), and it seems sometimes that she'd be just as happy partying in a gritty club in Bridgetown as she would swanking it up at a premiere or awards bash. Sure, catch her on autopilot and she'll trot out the kind of mature platitudes that her publicist probably loves, but which get us journos yawning big time, but when her guard's down, she's still the cheeky kid who likes to play around (her Twitter feed is a good example of the real Rihanna, if you can actually understand her often filthy slang).

In my brief time with her, at a gorgeous hotel in London that plays host to many a megastar, I think I'm seeing her at her most natural. My nerves are quickly replaced by awe at her grooming (blonde wig, fabulous eyelashes, daringly tight long dress – all of which, again, make her look older) and I'm determined to get glimpses of that girl who's found herself the most famous pop star on the planet. Some answers are admittedly a little too well rehearsed, but responses to questions about her future goals are endearingly all-over-the-shop; non-committal and laidback. Naturally she's not talking about her headline-hitting love life but I like to think that her casual attitude generally tells us plenty. In short, she's just enjoying herself. What's the problem with that? It's that chilled attitude that actually reveals more about her than any polished manifesto or monologue ever could. You see, she doesn't really have any insights because, in a nutshell, she's still too young to. *That's* the real Rihanna. By not claiming to be anything more than that young girl having a laugh (while plenty of pop stars her age, and younger, seem to believe they're the new Messiah) she's only making me like her all the more. And feel even older.

I'll always have Paris

I suppose I shouldn't have expected much. 'Holly – will you go and interview Paris Hilton for us please?' an editor casually emailed me one morning. I didn't need to be questioned twice. I'd actually always been kind of fascinated by the hotel-heiress/actress/singer/parfumier/fashion designer/(adult-)movie star.

The Simple Life, the TV show that she starred in with friend Nicole Richie, and which dumped these two spoilt brats into 'the real world' for laughs, was great hangover viewing on a Sunday. I figured that Paris must have had *something* about her to agree to it. There had to be a degree of self-awareness going on in her pretty little peroxide blonde head, surely?

Paris made her name on the early noughties party scene in New York, a 'celebutante' famous for being rich (her great-grandad founded the Hilton Hotel chain). A well-known relationship with Backstreet Boy Nick Carter and a rumoured one with Leonardo DiCaprio got her name out there even more. However, it was a sex-tape that made her infamous, a filmed liaison with randy 'it boy' and poker player Rick Salomon that got on to the web and became a phenomenon. (Rick's since gone on to marry a couple of times, once to *Beverly Hills 90210* star Shannen Doherty, and once to Pamela Anderson. Oh, he's a class act is Rick.)

To many, the way that Paris capitalised on her vacuousness, rather than any form of talent, was an insult to 'proper' entertainers. I kind of agree. Still, to deny her cultural status would be to sweep under the carpet an intriguing change in the showbiz world – a change that she's very much the Queen of. So while I had some questions about her pet chihuahua Tinkerbell (obviously) I also relished the chance to chat with someone who'd become an icon of a new era in celebrity. Everyone from Katie Price to Kim Kardashian owes her their living. Since Paris was about to release her debut album too, her move into the world of music would surely generate some juicy lines.

You'd think . . .

Paris took the word 'vacant' to new levels during our brief time together. My questions – quickly downgraded from the mildly intelligent as soon as it clicked what kind of a person I was dealing with – had to be repeated because she didn't understand them. Her answers, meanwhile, were so bland I practically fell into a coma right in front of her. She also insisted on using her highly forced catchphrase 'that's hot' at every given opportunity. Very annoying.

Unfortunately the outlet I'd be working for wasn't one that wanted a warts-and-all portrait of the great woman. They would actually be making a big deal out of Paris Hilton being in the pages of their frothy gossip mag, so being truly honest was obviously a no-no. To many of their readers, Paris was a role-model. As a freelancer just happy to get work I knew that I had no right to be the person to burst that bubble. I had to toe the line.

There is, however, a handy way around this. Sometimes phrases you read in an interview can seem positive enough, but to those in the know, all is not quite so rosy. After all, journalists should know how to manipulate the English language for their own satisfaction; it's part of our job. Hence, what a reader thinks a phrase means sometimes masks an entirely different emotion; something that, as objective reporters, we're really not meant to make public. Keep an eye out for some of these in your favourite mag or website and you'll see what I mean:

'She looked radiant' ACTUALLY MEANS 'She was caked in make-up'

'She was surprisingly laidback' ACTUALLY MEANS 'She turned up an hour late'

'She was effortlessly slim' ACTUALLY MEANS 'She's probably got an eating disorder'

'She's rushed off her feet with a busy schedule' ACTUALLY MEANS 'She's begging everyone for work'

Thus my finished article was littered with similarly carefully selected descriptions. You'd never have guessed my true opinion: that Paris boasted an extreme confidence (some would say arrogance) and the attitude that she was entitled to do anything she wanted. Why shouldn't she get an album deal? Or a fashion line? The fact that these came about because of the family she was born into, not because of hard work or skill, didn't seem to cross her mind. While I'm no hard lefty out to bash the rich, a little bit of humility from those more fortunate than us can go a long way to making up for any inequality. That afternoon, I saw none. For someone who seems to think everything around her is 'hot', she was . . . like . . . *totally* cold. Or, as I wrote in the article, 'serious and professional'.

Reality TV

As Paris Hilton found to her benefit, the single biggest change in the showbiz world since I started is the rise of what we call 'reality TV'.

One of the smash hit movies from my early days as a reporter was that Jim Carrey film *The Truman Show*. I went to the cinema to see it twice, I loved it so much. It's been several years since I've watched it now, though. That's not because it's suddenly become a bad movie – I still think it's Jim's best ever performance, certainly less wacky and shouty than we expect from him. No, I just haven't caught up with it recently because it simply doesn't seem that shocking any more. The plot about a guy being secretly filmed from birth, his life transmitted daily as a television show even while he has no idea everyone around him is an actor, doesn't just feel entirely believable these days, it actually feels dated. For a film that's supposed to be an exaggerated prophecy, that's a problem. I don't think anyone dared predict back when it came out that one day, the kind of 'reality entertainment' that Truman is unknowingly involved in would be a normal thing.

The more you watch reality TV, though, the more you realise that 'reality' is the last thing it is. While this new style of broadcasting might have originated from those 'fly on the wall' documentaries of the nineties, when we got as interested in regular people as we did soap characters (did anyone else love MTV's *The Real World*?), things have moved on significantly from the early days of offering some kind of truthful psychological insight. *Big Brother*, let's be honest, is no longer the social experiment that it claimed to be back when it was launched in 2000. Nowadays it's just a chance for us to laugh at a bunch of arrogant posers and wannabe glamour girls shouting at each other in a house for two months.

So over the years reality TV has morphed into an umbrella term for a host of different kinds of show, from talent competitions to documentary series to scary snapshots of orange people in Essex. Their only similarity – the fragile claim that they're all somehow authentic and truthful and we, as the audience, have the power to make winners out of this raw, fresh talent.

Hmmm . . . I'm not so sure. The people that actually have the power are those headline-hunting producers and editors who long ago cottoned on to the fact that while real life does produce *some* drama, manufactured life produces a hell of a lot more. Like puppeteers controlling their dolls, it's the behind-the-scenes teams that are really pulling the strings. And while some of these shows feature celebrities (and I use that term loosely) most use non-professionals dreaming of stardom who – crucially – don't have to get paid very much. Is it any wonder that this trend has completely enthralled a cash-strapped industry that likes to have total control over its stars?

I can't sit here and gripe though. I've spent more hours sat in front of the TV gawping at *The X Factor* and *Made in Chelsea* than Amy Childs has spent in the tanning booth. I love a lot of these shows. Like, *a lot*. They're easy, sensationalist TV and after a hard day at work, that's perfect escapism. It's just when they *become* work that I start to get depressed.

Here's what I mean. A skilful production team can make a no-hoper on a reality show seem like the most hilarious and lovable person you're ever likely to meet. After all, it's the programme makers' job to ensure their characters are fun to watch and keep us hooked. It's no different to creating *Coronation Street* or *EastEnders*. Put those reality stars on a red carpet, though, no longer protected by producers and writers crafting their image, and it's then that you see proper reality. The fact is, so many of these manufactured stars have nothing to say. Like, nada. Why would they? They're fame-hungry wannabes who've experienced very little in life and whose main focus is on themselves. Forced into an interview situation with them and all they're able to talk about are the faked minutiae of their fairly average lives. That's fine in moderation. But the entertainment world – especially film premieres – has become so awash with these people these days, you think yourself lucky now to come away from an interview with anything approaching insight. I've lost count of the number of celebrity events I've been to in a professional capacity, hoping to get a good story from a genuine star, but have ended up with just a few lines of small talk from a Jasmine Lennard, a Brian Belo or an Aisleyne Horgan-Wallace. Reality TV is the small screen's biggest innovation in my lifetime and there's a lot of great stuff that's arisen from it. But creating a host of new Stephen Frys isn't one of them.

Trying to be level-headed, I probably wouldn't want to turn back the clock and live in a world where we'd never sampled reality TV. There's simply been too many iconic showbiz moments that have come from it – from Jade Goody admitting to not knowing that America is an English-speaking country on *Big Brother* to Susan Boyle shocking everyone on *Britain's Got Talent* – for me to discredit the genre entirely. I also truly believe that the people who genuinely have something to offer will last the distance, rather than just the few months after their show has ended. Jade is a great example. She might not have been a great wit or creative powerhouse, but in a media world full of waffling experts and the endlessly opinionated, her down-to-earth attitude and no-nonsense personality were like a warm cuddle. *That* was her talent. You could argue the same for Stacey Solomon, certainly more famous for her smile and inadvertent one-liners than for her singing. One of the joys of reality shows is that, every now and then, someone like these two comes along – a person who is endlessly fascinating and appealing simply by being themselves. When the final months of Jade's battle with cervical cancer were documented in a series of programmes on Sky Living in 2009, some said that it was reality TV going too far. But with Jade, someone who had lived so much of her adult life in front of reality TV cameras, it actually felt right. The small screen was her home. It made sense to chronicle her death using the medium where she truly came to life. On 22 March 2009 when she lost her fight, even the most hard-hearted of us shed a tear.

This said, when you're standing in the freezing cold for hours on end, rammed into a tiny pen with umpteen other tired and bored journalists, patiently waiting for someone exciting to walk up the red carpet, and all you get is Katie Price talking about her latest book that was ghost-written for her . . . well, that's something different. It's then that you find yourself thinking back to the days when famous people were actually famous because they'd done something more than just let a camera crew follow them around. Complete access to your life doesn't in itself make you intriguing; that requires real star quality. You've either got it or you haven't.

Adele

Thankfully there are still some people who are pretty much the polar opposite of vacuous reality TV stars . . .

February 2013. Adele's just won an Oscar and I'm asked to write an article about her rise to fame. Yes, *another* one. There is a huge amount of celebrities out there, but there's still only a finite number of angles you can take. Childhood, heartbreak, happiness, weight gain, weight loss and baby joy – I've covered them all several times over. You know how some TV shows, after they come back after an advert break, recap everything that happened in part one, as if our memories are so short we can't remember what was going on ten minutes ago? Sometimes I feel that my job is just constant recapping of celebrities' personal lives.

Adele doesn't make it easy for us either. As much as I might want to track down exclusives about her life, she opts for the old-fashioned route of letting her amazing music do the talking (her minimal, and now legendary, performance of 'Someone Like You' at the 2011 BRIT Awards is a case in point). You won't find endless interviews with her or shed-loads of paparazzi shots, like you would many of her fellow starlets. Someone like Kim Kardashian relies on the press regurgitating intimate stories about her because there's no real end product, like an album or a movie, to speak for her. Adele, on the other hand, wouldn't even reveal her child's name to the media for weeks (thank God it wasn't really called Peanut). Such modesty is unusual in today's climate, but few could deny that it seems to have worked so far. So while I'd give my only pair of Louboutins for an interview with her, I also know that, actually, I don't want her to change. Her refusal is exactly what makes her so damn cool.

The fact that there are many stars who really don't need us showbiz journalists to shout about them is a realisation that everyone in my job has at some point in their career. I don't mind feeling useless, though. Actually it's healthy to be reminded that, in a world driven by hype and spin, sometimes simplicity can still win the day. When it comes to being a music icon with millions of sales, it can just be as basic as having great tunes. Or, for a respected actor, great performances. At the same Oscars ceremony as Adele, Daniel Day-Lewis won a record-breaking third Best Actor award. He's a bona fide god but keeps his life totally private. So far from feeling worthless, I actually find it very heartening that substance *can* win over style.

Just take a look at this list of the UK's biggest selling albums of all time (at the time of writing) for extra proof:

1. Queen – *Greatest Hits*

2. Abba – *Gold*

3. The Beatles – *Sgt. Pepper's Lonely Hearts Club Band*

4. Oasis – *What's the Story, Morning Glory?*

5. Adele – *21*

6. Michael Jackson – *Thriller*

7. Dire Straits – *Brothers in Arms*

8. Pink Floyd – *The Dark Side of the Moon*

9. Michael Jackson – *Bad*

10. Queen – *Greatest Hits II*

Queen, Michael Jackson, Pink Floyd, Dire Straits – all acts who not only feature heavily in my dad's CD collection but who were also known as much for their privacy as their music. Freddie Mercury's secret life only really became known after his untimely death in 1991. Michael Jackson's is still a mystery, four years down the line from his. All the surviving members of Dire Straits and Pink Floyd, meanwhile, could happily hobble down the high street with their Zimmer frames without getting bothered (though all, presumably, with bank accounts that are fit to burst).

Of course, it's true that pretty much any act needs publicity to get off the ground. The whole 'girl next door' approach from Adele has been just as much a selling point as Rihanna's endless saucy photo shoots or Lady Gaga's much-discussed weirdness. But just how much a celebrity courts publicity as the years go on varies hugely. Sometimes, as that cheesy old Ronan Keating song goes, 'You say it best when you say nothing at all.' Coming from someone like me that makes a living from stars wanting to talk, that may sound odd but it's true. The most exciting acts are the ones – like Adele – with an air of mystery, who worry more about choruses than column inches. They might make my life bloody difficult but really, I love them for it.

Los Angeles

If ever you want to feel insecure, go to LA.

I've been a few times. Once, to meet with publicists and tell them why they should be giving the magazine I was writing for some exclusives with their clients. I was there for a whole week, my mornings spent in offices chatting to skinny Valley Girls about their movie stars, my afternoons spent by the hotel pool trying not to feel too fat. A couple of the meetings resulted in good material coming my way so it was worth it, but Los Angeles has a way of playing with your mind. Out there, in the show business capital of the world, you quickly realise just how small a fish you are in the giant showbiz ocean. In London, I've worked my way up the ladder and industry people know who I am. In LA, the only thing big about me is my arse.

It wasn't until the second time that I went out to Los Angeles that this pecking order became most painfully obvious. I was there to cover The Academy Awards, known to us all as the Oscars. Watch them on the TV and what you see are the stars, those gorgeous gods and goddesses preened to perfection, laughing and back-slapping as they enjoy what's essentially their annual office party – albeit in outfits that cost more than my annual wage. It looks an amazing night, right?

What you don't see so much of is the *other* side of the velvet rope. My side. Yes, we reporters have to dress up too, but unfortunately our outfits aren't ever going to be splashed all over the front pages. In fact, when you're back in your hotel room trying to edit a piece for the website, a tight strapless LBD is the last thing you want to be wearing.

Oscar night is chaos: the waiting, the shouting, the being completely ignored by megastars. Yes it's warmer than a premiere night in London, but at least in my own city, I'm just one of a handful of reporters. At the Academy Awards in LA, it's you versus the rest of the world. Unless you're Ryan Seacrest, the chances of you getting to have a matey chat with Sandra or Reese are very small.

I was there when *The King's Speech* triumphed, a relatively small British movie taking on the big boys. One of the editors I work for thought, quite rightly, that we shouldn't be five and a half thousand miles away from LA, covering who wore what frocks from the comfort of our London office. That year a reporter should be in Hollywood itself trying to get an interview with Colin Firth. As someone who'd fancied him ever since *Pride and Prejudice* made my Sunday nights as a teenager significantly more interesting, I wasn't going to complain when I was luckily chosen to be the one. Quite the opposite, in fact: I had butterflies in my stomach from the moment I booked my flight. Come Oscars evening, a warm Sunday night in February, I was properly hyper. My job was to calmly supply the website with A-List gossip and interviews but standing on the red carpet, as jet lag mingled with feelings of responsibility, I struggled to even control my breathing. Finally, I heard his arrival. Screams of 'Colin! Colin!' rippled up the avenue of snappers and fans outside the Kodak Theatre and there, in the distance, a tall figure in black began his long walk. After what seemed a lifetime, finally he was within reach. 'Colin!' I shouted out to him, his shape now recognisable as the upper-class eye candy from *Bridget Jones* and *Love, Actually*. 'A word for your British fans.'

And there, suddenly, Mr Darcy was stood in front of me, smiling and dapper in his Tom Ford suit. A publicist was permanently on his arm, edging him ever onwards down the carpet but for a brief minute he belonged to me (well, to me and to the three other reporters who stuck their microphones in his face when I started interviewing him). In a maelstrom of hungry showbiz hacks on the busiest night of their year, I momentarily felt very special. The questions and answers might have been predictable – Me: 'How do you rate your chances of winning?' Col: 'Oh, I'm just glad to be here', etc., etc. – but few could deny that there was something special in the air that night. A tingle.

And then, a couple of hours later, he won an Oscar. It was a great moment for the British film industry, of course, but all of a sudden, my polite, slightly nervy pre-awards chat no longer had much currency. Now he was a winner I needed an update, a conversation with King Colin, the newly crowned monarch of the night. How did it feel? Had you prepared your speech? Will you be keeping the award in your downstairs loo in Chiswick?

My earlier bonding with the man, I presumed, could only stand me in good stead as I waited for him again later that night. When the awards ceremony had begun earlier in the evening, some journalists with the right credentials had headed into the theatre's backstage area to attend the mini press conferences given by the winners straight after they walked off stage with their Oscar. I had a different plan. I'd jumped into a cab and headed down North Highland Avenue then on to West Sunset Boulevard, past the infamous Chateau Marmont and on to the Art Deco elegance of the Sunset Tower Hotel where the legendary *Vanity Fair* party was taking place. This was one of the hottest bashes in town (Sir Elton

John's legendary Oscar night knees-up being the other one) and anyone who's anyone turned up. Here I would get my follow-up interview with the man of the moment.

Just like earlier in the evening, minutes now seemed like hours as we waited for the stars to arrive. And just like earlier, Colin's name was chanted maniacally at the far end of the red carpet as soon as he arrived, Oscar clutched in his right hand. I got my camera guy – a Californian called Drew who, judging from the chats in our downtime, didn't appear to have watched any films, ever – ready and primed.

Once again Colin edged ever closer and with a sense of déjà vu I began shouting out his name, along with the magic words 'British press!' I naïvely presumed it would have the same effect as before.

This time, however, Mr Firth remained not so much at arm's length, more a good 20 feet away. I turned up the volume of my hollering, as did the gaggle of British morning TV crews stood next to me. He waved. He posed for a few photos with Anne Hathaway, also arriving for the party at the same time. He said a few cursory words to people that weren't me. Then . . . he went into the party. The end.

Drew, ever the diplomat, said in his local drawl: 'Well, that guy was a douche.' While I disagreed – nothing could taint my opinion of Colin – my place in the pecking order had been painfully reiterated. Stars rarely like talking to the press but if they absolutely *have* to then they might. I saw that on the way in, when Colin was just one of several nominees and needed to be noticed. But if they don't need the publicity any more – for example, if they've just gone and won an actual Oscar – then forget it. We are not their friends.

I don't blame Colin Firth. He was having his biggest night ever and unsurprisingly wanted to go and let his hair down and sink a few glasses of Cristal. He didn't have to do anything he didn't want. But that's the problem with the Oscars for reporters who aren't big stars themselves (like the aforementioned Mr Seacrest, or the red carpet legend that is Joan Rivers). You can wait hours for an interview and then . . . nothing. Ultimately, it's a night for the movie industry, not the media. If the movie industry doesn't feel like letting you into its world for a couple of minutes, even seconds, then it doesn't have to.

So when you next watch the ceremony on the television and see all the British press out there, don't presume we're hanging out with the stars. When the news anchorman crosses to his reporter out in LA, dolled up to the nines in her posh ball gown, and he says something like: 'Here's Helen, partying with the rich and famous,' remember that he doesn't *actually* know what he's talking about. There's no 'hanging out' or 'partying'. There's mainly a lot of waiting, a lot of shouting and a lot of celebrities waving from a distance as they keep their own world very much private from ours.

Technology

I didn't get into this job to become a technical boffin. I just wanted to speak to talented entertainers and hopefully find out what makes them tick. Unfortunately to record talented entertainers telling you what makes them tick, you need technology. And just as I get comfortable with one system, along comes another to screw everything up again. When I started this job, all I needed was a dictaphone to capture the conversation. Since then, with journalists no longer being just 'print' or 'broadcast' but having to multi-task with a variety of outlets, the kit I carry with me has changed significantly. The audio/visual pros and cons of each are endlessly debated by the tech boys at work but really I'm not that bothered. I just want something I can carry in my handbag.

Place your tape recorder (I still call it that, despite actual 'tape' having been phased out years ago) on the table between you and your interviewee and the last thing you want is for it to go wrong. Consider the number of interviews I do, however, and simple maths tells you technology has got to cock up sometimes.

My technique for dealing with such mechanical blunders is simply to keep quiet. A famous actor or singer really doesn't want to think about trying to fix a corrupted hard disk. I don't mind admitting that, on some occasions, I've been aware that my kit has gone wrong early on in an interview, yet I've continued to carry on with things as if nothing had happened. So I'm sat there with someone giving me beautifully crafted answers, knowing full well that the only place those answers are being stored is in my head. By the time I come to transcribing them they've usually got jumbled up with mental notes to pick up the dry cleaning and buy some more toilet rolls and are pretty useless. Fortune has, on the whole, been kind to me, though. When such breakdowns occur it's usually been during an interview with a dull director or co-star, someone I'm only speaking to because so many film junkets are 'all or nothing' set-ups. If you want the megastar, you have to do the nobodies too.

The biggest name to fall victim of one of my technical hitches was Natalie Portman. This was not one of those interviews that I could write off to experience – I really needed her words. My equipment at the time, however, felt differently, and out of the blue it had simply died on me in less than two minutes. I kept going with the interview, though; confessing would achieve nothing. I simply smiled, nodded and desperately fought back the tears.

She was on great form too. She talked openly and eloquently about the pressure of finding fame aged 13 and the crazy world of trying to balance education with growing up in the spotlight. In her adult life, Natalie has gone from appearing in *Star Wars* to studying at Harvard, quite a career shift, and we'd laughed about her appeal among the sci-fi fans in her Psychology class at Uni. All relaxed, chatty, great stuff. And only the first 84 seconds of it recorded.

It was only as my time came to an end that the gravity of my situation hit me. I was in America, paid for by the film company and scheduled to fly back later that night. This was not some unknown director in London whose words I really didn't need. Natalie was going to be a thousand-word article.

Once I'd said my 'thank yous' and 'goodbyes', I subtly slid over to the publicist in charge, whispering as calmly as possible that the interview they'd spent weeks setting up for me was a non-starter. 'It must have been the X-ray machine at the airport that messed up the electrics,' I suggested (I have no idea whether this is even possible but this was a PR girl I was speaking to, not Stephen Hawking. I figured she'd know even less about this stuff than I did). I know it's a bad workman that blames his tools, but I wasn't in the mood to be forgiving. I needed some sympathy and, more importantly, some more time with Natalie.

'Uh huh,' said the tall, Courteney Cox lookalike. She was clad in regulation PR black and had a non-committal look on her face that could have either been the result of time spent rehearsing a professional expression to ward off over-eager journalists or, more likely, Botox.

'Mmmm-kay,' she continued. 'We could probably squeeze you back in a couple hours. For, like, five minutes. Can you get some more equipment by then?'

I was gone before she'd even finished her speech, out on to the streets of the Big Apple to find an overpriced electrical shop that could flog a desperate tourist something on which to record an interview with a future Oscar winner. These days I could have easily recorded straight on to my phone or tablet, but this was in the early noughties, just before the MP3 revolution reached journalism. So, while I might have been armed back then with 2002's latest mobile and laptop, I could just as soon record on to them as fly to the moon. No, what I was in need of that day was called a minidisc recorder. I won't blame you if you've never heard of them. Back then, minidiscs were supposed to be the future. The fact that they're now virtually forgotten shows that such a prediction didn't quite happen. Still, back then they were the height of technical fashion, and an hour later – and $200 lighter – I was back in the hotel, carefully filing away the receipt for a new minidisc player for expenses. Our finance department was made up of stingy bean counters straight out of a Charles Dickens tale, so this was going to be interesting.

The new recorder did its job and I got the interview with Natalie Portman. Again. If I ever needed proof that stars on the promotional trail are frequently just on autopilot, not really taking in what's going on, then that second interview was it. There I was, back in the same room as before, wearing the same outfit (albeit with more of a flush in my cheeks after my sprint around the city looking for the Manhattan equivalent of Dixons) and asking pretty much the same questions as before. Did Natalie say anything? Of course not. On a junket day, actors do so many interviews that all the journalists start to look the same anyway. When one of those journalists actually *is* the same as one earlier, it's not even going to register. Frankly though, I wasn't looking for recognition. I just needed a repeat of what I'd got earlier, all that great chat about puberty and stardom and college.

An afternoon, however, is a long time in junket world. After hours chatting to the press it seemed that Natalie was, understandably, getting tired. Sure she was still as sweet and lovely and annoyingly pretty as before. But as for opening up? I'd missed my moment. The revelations train, it seemed, had left the station. The material I got this second time wasn't half as good as before. I left America relieved that I'd at least got something from the interview but frustrated to know that it could have been so much better.

On the plus side, I did get the money back for the new piece of kit. It even became part of the office equipment pool for the next few months, sitting in a drawer ready to be used at a moment's notice should one of us reporters head out on a story. Then, just as I became confident that I knew what nearly all the buttons did, the tech boys decided to upgrade to a new system and it was consigned to the dustbin of history. 'This new gear is so easy to use,' the chief computer geek announced excitedly to the office during one morning meeting. 'Even Holly couldn't break it.'

Bruce Willis

In my very early days as a reporter, I scored an interview with one of the biggest movie stars in the world – Bruce Willis. It didn't exactly go to plan. While I initially blamed my own inexperience, looking back (and with the benefit of having met Bruce several times since), I think the fault was actually his not mine. The simple fact is, he doesn't really like doing interviews. If he's in an uncooperative mood, there's not much you can do about it.

It was on the bottom floor of his Planet Hollywood restaurant in London that Bruce had deigned to give a handful of reporters a few minutes of his afternoon. In between promotional activities for the glorified burger bar (which has since stuttered financially and Bruce is no longer involved with) he also had a film to plug. There was an odd mood from the start, publicists hovering nervously in every corner of the dimly lit basement, the atmosphere sterile and strained. I waited my turn, anxiously rehearsing my questions in my head so as not to waste a precious second of the three minutes I would be spending with the *Die Hard* star. Yes – three whole minutes. I'd had conversations with bus drivers that lasted longer.

My name called, I walked up to the diner-style booth where Bruce was sat. The megastar looked miserable. Sitting down next to him, I started up my friendly chat: 'Hi Mr Willis, my name's Holly—' at the *exact* moment one of his 'people' marched over and plonked down some food in front of him. Wow, I thought. I'm sure being made to feel like Bruce really wants me here.

Bruce looked at the sustenance laid out for him. It wasn't just any snack. Oh no. Here was probably the least action hero kind of food you can imagine. Bruce, it seemed, didn't want a nice bloody steak or an All American hotdog, the kind of hearty, meaty fast food you'd expect him to chomp on while saving the world from an asteroid.

Bruce wanted a mug of soup.

And what's more, he wanted to *really* think about seasoning and stirring and sipping this cup of soup for the whole duration of the interview, precisely the time I'd have much preferred him to be giving me some great insights on what it was like being in another movie where he gets to blow loads of stuff up. The result? I get a three-minute interview with Bruce where his answers are all monotonous and half-hearted, like his mind is somewhere else. It was. It was thinking about chunky vegetables.

'So, Bruce. Lovely to chat to you here in the surroundings of your very own restaurant. But, of course, it's not all about that at the moment for you because you've got a new film out. Tell me why did you want to play this role? What was the attraction?'

'Well, you know . . . *SLURP* . . . It was just a . . . *SLURP* . . . great script . . . *SLURP*'

'Er . . . Okay then. It's interesting that your daughter Rumer is now getting into movies too. She's certainly following in the family tradition! Are you and her mum the kind of parents to give her advice, seeing as you both know the business so well? There's not a lot of kids out there who could boast a family that understands Hollywood so well.'

'Well, y'know . . . *ADDS SALT TO SOUP* . . . *ADDS PEPPER

TO SOUP* . . . *STIRS SOUP* . . . *SLURPS SOUP* . . . She's a smart kid. She knows the deal.'

I'm guessing you get the idea . . .

I was tempted to mention Bruce's ill-fated eighties pop career to see if that would get his attention.

I've caught up with Bruce Willis when he's not been waylaid with jet lag or craving soup and it's a *very* different experience. Twinkle-eyed and cool, he's more of the cheeky chappy that movie fans so love him for being. Still, even on those occasions there's a definite sensation of the world revolving around him. He's in charge of things, not you. When your movies have grossed around $3 billion at the box office I guess you've earned the right to call the shots but it makes the moment an email arrives, inviting you to the new Willis junket, a tense one. Which Bruce will I get this time? The superstar or the *souper* star?

Child stars

Child stars are a mixed blessing for a showbiz journo. On the one hand, their inevitable growing up in public provides us with lots of headlines, whether it's by simply looking radiant in a grown-up gown at a premiere or, more sleazily, by ending up in rehab. On the other hand, though, child stars can be a pain in the bum when you actually have to meet them. There's nothing quite so disconcerting as having to suck up to someone young enough to be your own child and who's got more ego than a heavyweight champion (despite only being four foot six).

That said, not every child star is the same. The British ones are generally a more restrained bunch, public school-educated and excessively well mannered. With our movie and TV industry's endless period dramas there's plenty of opportunity for nice middle-class kids to play a Dickens or Austen adolescent before heading off to Hollywood to politely emulate Carey and Kate. And supporting them all the way are their well-bred parents, scions of the Home Counties and longtime Volvo drivers, keeping their kiddies in check should signs of brattish behaviour ever start brewing.

Then there are the Americans. Our cousins across the Atlantic have never exactly been known for their shy and retiring nature and their child stars only prove the point. To hear a 14-year-old Californian talk about their 'brand' and 'crossover potential' without any irony is disconcerting to say the least, evidence of a culture so at home with the business aspect of entertainment that children are experts before they're even old enough to open a bank account. It's accompanying these kind of kids that we see the more stereotypical version of the 'pushy parent', that failed performer who – now too old to find fame themselves – wants to try all over again through their child.

The trouble is, teenage rebellion is a natural phase. It's not something you can repress, however famous you are and however much those around you might try. Of course, if you're a regular tenth grader then the odd argument with your parents or puff on a cigarette is hardly going to be breaking news. If you're a multi-millionaire with a six-album contract on the other hand, what for many is simple self-discovery often gets blown out of all proportion.

Drew Barrymore starred in *E.T.*, once the biggest film of all time, when she was seven. By 14 she was a smoker, drinker and cocaine addict with two spells in rehab under her belt (the nude *Playboy* shoot was still to come). Then there is Macaulay Culkin, the first child actor to earn $1 million a movie after his success in *Home Alone* as a 10-year-old. By 16 he was seeking legal emancipation from his parents in order to gain control of his earnings. The noughties saw the rise of the Olsen Twins – Mary-Kate and Ashley – stars of US TV show *Full House* since they were teething, reportedly amassing a $137 million fortune from films and merchandising by the time they were 18. That was also when Mary-Kate was admitted into hospital with anorexia.

Admittedly it's not always about age. Fame and money do funny things to people, whether they're five or ninety-five, but impose the weird bubble of celebrity around someone so young that they're still trying to get to grips with the world and the results will only be all the more devastating, especially without a trustworthy support system. Should I ever have littl'uns who want to get on the stage I'll be making sure it's done with the utmost care and sensitivity. There's definitely a case for making them study the collected works of Keira Knightley for inspiration, rather than the life and loves of Lindsay Lohan.

Luckily child stars grow into adults. Many's the former teenage megastar who now, as a grown-up, has a more philosophical and open-minded view on life than someone who didn't have such crazy experiences as a kid. Would Ryan Gosling now be making thoughtful, intriguing, challenging movies had he not spent two years on the Disney Channel's *Mickey Mouse Club* in the early nineties, alongside Britney and Christina?

I doubt it. Sometimes growing up proves a challenge – just look at Michael Jackson. Often though, like Ryan and Drew, the former teen star's segue into adulthood is filled with wisdom beyond years.

Of course, it will never cease to be a shock when a child star turn into someone ... well ... sexy. When I first interviewed Justin Bieber it was just a few months after his debut record. I'd travelled across London to the hotel where he was staying, a place that was blatantly obvious from miles away thanks to the army of fans waiting outside for a glimpse of their poster boy. I use the word 'army' deliberately. Judging by the banners and T-shirts this crowd of girls were rocking, all declaring undying love, they'd head fearlessly into a warzone if Justin asked them to. Talk about building up my hopes. To these girls who had camped for hours to secure their place, Justin was a god. I could barely imagine what meeting such a messianic figure would be like.

I can tell you very simply what it was like: it was like interviewing a child. A child with cute floppy hair, maybe. A child with huge amounts of YouTube hits to his name, it's true. But still a child. As I tried to chat to him he didn't pay me much attention. Now I don't think this was because he was an inherently bad person or anything. It's just because he was a kid with a kid's wandering mind. Everyone around him was telling him how amazing he was (because, to be blunt, he was making them a lot of money), but he lacked the adult experience to deal with it in a focused way. If I'd had thousands of fans endlessly screaming my name before I'd even hit puberty, I'm sure I'd have been the same.

The last time he was in the UK, though? Wow. New hair. New body. New attitude. In reality it was still only a couple of years since our first meeting, but that time had seen him change significantly. God bless hormones. The fans were still outside the hotel, as before, and his entourage was still as big. But this time . . . Is it wrong to say I kind of fancied him? After much consideration and discussion with friends, I don't think so. After all, guys I know think the same about Emma Watson and no one bats an eyelid. With his new-found chiselled jaw, stronger frame and – crucially – the ability to deal with a grown-up interview, all of a sudden I could kind of understand exactly what those passionate fans were on about. He *had* something.

I wasn't at the gig more recently where he kept fans waiting for over an hour before he appeared on stage, but such treatment of your audience does suggest there's still a bit more growing up to do on his part. I don't think his upset fans will truly desert him though. I know I'm not going to. With those looks the Bieb could get away with murder. You see, gaining wisdom beyond your years might be one of the advantages of being a former child star but growing up into someone really fit is probably an even bigger one.

Middle Age

The most difficult type of person to interview? It's not a genre of performer – actor, singer, dancer, etc. It's a gender and an age group:

The middle-aged woman.

Do I feel good about writing these words? Of course not, yet this is the situation. With the way that showbiz works, it's no wonder that when a woman hits 45 plus she can start to go a bit doolally. Simply put, the game doesn't play out in the favour of women of a certain age. Guys are allowed to grow old, get wrinkles, show off their salt-and-pepper hair and be deemed 'distinguished'. When a woman occasionally does the same, stripping herself of make-up and airbrushing for a gimmicky photo shoot she's patronisingly deemed 'brave', while causing a media storm and a flurry of debate (such as when forty-something legend Jamie Lee Curtis did it for an issue of US mag *More* in 2002). All that *just for wearing no slap*. Then, after a few weeks, whaddya know . . .? Everything just goes back to how it was. Men are allowed to age. Women aren't.

Take Madonna. Here's a woman who made her name by setting the pace, working one step ahead of the crowd by being true to herself. Her image constantly changes, while dabbling with everything from acting to fashion made her a cutting-edge sex symbol for 20-odd years. Yet when she hit 50, attitudes in the media really changed. On the one hand, she was deemed embarrassing for still making pop music and wanting to work with artists and producers half her age. On the other, any signs of her middle age – specifically her wrinkled hands – were given the kind of obsessive press attention normally reserved for a warring dictator. If she can't be young at heart, but she's also not allowed to show her age, what the hell is she meant to do? Is it any wonder that she can sometimes be deemed 'difficult' to interview?

Meanwhile boys of the same era – Paul Weller, Prince, Bruce Springsteen – are allowed to seamlessly carry on doing what they've been doing since they were teenagers and, in the process, get nothing but praise. Madge dressing up as a cheerleader aged 54 might not exactly be my idea of dignified, but is it any less dignified than middle-aged dads still playing the rock star?

The movie world is no different. As Johnny Depp (born 1963), Liam Neeson (born 1952) and Robert Downey Jr (born 1965) are finding that every producer in town wants them to be a sexy leading man, contemporaries such as Nicole Kidman (born 1967) and Halle Berry (born 1966) – both of whom have won more Oscars than those boys – are finding interesting roles in mainstream movies extremely hard to come by. Analysts might argue that films starring middle-aged women aren't box-office gold, but if we're not trying to make them, how do we know? Check out a list of Hollywood's biggest leading ladies of the eighties and nineties and it reads like a 'Where are they now?' article. Jessica Lange, Michelle Pfeiffer, Sharon Stone, Geena Davis, Diane Lane, Kathleen Turner . . . They must all be loitering patiently in their Beverly Hills mansions, waiting to officially be deemed 'old ladies' so that they can start getting all those 'mad Granny' supporting roles that Hollywood so loves. But if you're in your fifties, there's pretty much nothing.

In one working week I saw this situation at its most blatant. On one day I went to interview an award-winning middle-aged actress, someone actually known for her cheery breeziness on screen and of whom I was a massive fan. She was a *nightmare*. She seemed to inherently distrust me from the word go, despite my line of questioning hardly being controversial. When my recording gear wasn't on I felt like the Invisible Woman, this star totally speaking 'through' me to her publicist. When our chat was being recorded she was, at best, guarded. At her worst, she was just plain rude.

Of course, I was annoyed by her behaviour, but then, later that week, a TV producer friend of mine told me over a drink how the entertainment show she was working on had been ordered to drop an interview with Julianne Moore because she was deemed 'too old'. Forget the fact that she's one of the most respected actresses in the world and all that . . . With so many corners of the media treating 'mature' women like that, I thought, suddenly my interviewee seeming pissed off with the world made complete sense.

Which brings me back to my first point. Celebrity women of a certain age can be difficult in interviews because, understandably, they find themselves struggling with the press and their careers in a way that guys would simply never have to. Constantly being analysed for their looks, endlessly having to look over their shoulders as a new sexy young thing works her way up the ranks – it's enough to shatter anyone's ego. So as a journalist wanting an easy time I hardly relish the prospect of interviewing these ladies; but as a fellow woman who understands how society's perception of me changes with each birthday, I'm on their side. Insecurity isn't a pleasant thing to have to spend your time with but I'm a hell of a lot more sympathetic to it than I am sexism and ageism.

I Am Cynic

One night recently I turned down a glass of wine offered by a publicist friend, because I'm trying not to drink midweek. When you're at events almost every night, finding yourself sinking numerous servings of free wine of an evening is all too easy. Just when you think you've got to the bottom of your glass, up pops a handsome waiter ready to refill. It was early January, and I'd worked out that during the Christmas season I was averaging around 40 units a week, more than I could ever bear to admit to my GP. Definitely time for a break. However, while I could cope with that, my PR pal wasn't so positive:

'What kind of journalist are you?' came her shocked reply. 'A reporter that doesn't drink? At least you're still cynical. You've still got a bit of media in you.'

She seemed relieved, as if she was trying to justify her own beliefs by making sure I still fitted neatly into a box – a box marked 'typical hack'. Just as we journalists have our own view of the PR world, the publicists have their own view of us too. As relationships go, it's a bit like that of a pop duo who don't really get on but who both realise that the other is their meal ticket. They're a lot more successful working as a pair than individually. So if one of you shows signs of straying from the accepted path, alarm bells start ringing.

But she was right – I *do* still have a cynical edge. Along with a pickled liver and feet sore from high heels, cynicism is one of the major traits of any showbiz journalist. I guess we've all just seen too much hype in our lives to be any other way. And unlike alcohol, there are no government limits to help us cut back.

Cynicism develops gradually, partly because of the cyclical nature of the showbiz world. Work in the entertainment arena for a couple of years and you'll really see the pattern. Television has its seasons just as predictably as nature; *The X Factor* at the end of August signalling that summer is nearly over, while November's *I'm A Celebrity* . . . launch tells you that Christmas is on the way. Then there's the film world: awards season running from November to March, rom-coms usually getting released at Easter, summer blockbusters from May, not to mention animations during every school holiday. Even music has its calendar, the New Year a time for credible new artists to launch off the back of all those 'Ones to Watch' features every January, while late autumn signals the biggest album releases of the year, all hoping to cash in on the festive market. Of course, most businesses have a regular timetable, but somehow when it's entertainment, because it's an industry we like to think of as spontaneous and fun, it always seems more disappointing to discover that actually it's as ruthlessly calculated as mobile phone tariffs.

Then there are those moments when you're reading an interview with a star that you've recently met yourself, and they've given exactly the same answers to this journalist as they did to you. Even the supposedly ad-libbed jokes are the same. At a premiere I once heard Will Ferrell do the same joke to every outlet that he was interviewed by – it was just after the World Cup and he had turned up on the red carpet in an England football strip, supposedly unaware that the tournament was over. During each interview an assistant would whisper in his ear and he would then theatrically proclaim: 'Whaaaat?! Why did no one tell me the football's finished?' Funny the first time. Not the sixth. With reporters simply expected to go along with such a stunt, just as we're meant to go along to the same showbiz events at the same time every year, how could you not get cynical? For the first couple of years of my career, I was blithely sucked in by it all, still innocent to the subtleties of the game. By year three, repetition had begun to beat me down.

Such cynicism can affect every aspect of your work. '*Why* is this person being so nice to me?' you find yourself worrying. 'Just what is it that they're hiding?' I know of journalists more vengeful than myself who have for years been trying to find some dirt on seemingly happy and mellow stars precisely for the reason that, to them, they just seem *too* settled. Will Smith, for example. As a well-known charmer and funny man, many of the more sensationalist hacks are convinced Big Willy is only super sweet because he's hiding something. Why else would he be so friendly, other than to hide his secret life as Satan worshipper or his penchant for dressing up in women's clothing?

Here's a radical suggestion, colleagues: maybe he's just genuinely content? Unfortunately, being 'genuinely content' isn't a story.

Rumours of an open marriage and even flirtations with Scientology have occasionally flitted around Will, but they've never really come to anything. The Smith household carries on in most of our minds as a regular and happy place. Personally speaking, I've met the former Fresh Prince several times and can only confirm that he truly seems to be a lovely bloke; satisfied with his lot but also enthusiastic about moving forward. Many stars seem to be slightly troubled with their need to perform, fighting a battle between those more extrovert tendencies and a conflicting inner personality that struggles with such showing off. Too often it's a face-off that ends up with the confused star checking into rehab.

Not Will Smith, though. Even in his time as a rapper he was chirpy and jokey rather than angry and gangster. He just seems to love everything about performing and, as a result, he is a pleasure to spend time with. In a one-to-one interview he treats you like you're the most important person in the world. In a press conference he plays to the crowd, entertaining like a master. I'd argue that it's impossible not to love him. Unfortunately, for the more hardened in my profession, that love is similar to my dream of being teetotal: just not good enough.

Still, cynicism is something that I'm really trying to give up (like white wine). It's easy to laugh at Hollywood stars with their New Age platitudes and smiley outlooks honed by hours of therapy but I sometimes wish I could be that positive. It should be no surprise that you'll find me every Sunday down at my local Pilates class, trying to ground myself and focus on the good things after a week of such muck-raking. It's crucial to remember what's really important in life (I tell myself as I wobble about on a giant exercise ball). Then, before you know it, you're back in the Monday-morning rush, blinded by work and lost in showbiz all over again.

Watching films

Just as breaking a story before anyone else gives me a thrill, so does seeing a movie first. It's sad but true. During my early career, it felt wonderfully cheeky to leave the office at, say, two in the afternoon and head into town to see a new blockbuster at a special press preview screening – *and* get paid for it. But it was and is still part of the job. If I'm going to interview the star of the movie at a premiere, junket or press conference then it's only fair to them that I've actually seen what they've spent the last few months of their life working on. Film companies insist on it. In fact, on the rare occasions you're allowed to do an interview *without* having watched the movie you know that there's a simple explanation: the film's so bad producers don't want the media to see it.

I know that I won't have this privilege for ever, so I'm not ashamed to enjoy it while I can. I've got a number of friends in the business who look after me well, but I'm not naïve enough to think that those perks would carry on if I ever changed career. I could hang up my laptop for good on a Friday and I know that by the time Monday comes around I'd be off a whole bunch of mailing lists. It's important to relish it while you're still allowed to.

Even after all these years, my family continues to find it funny when I describe what I've been doing recently and include going to the cinema as 'work'. But by the time I'm stood outside the cinema and am focusing on what Gerard Butler or Robert Pattinson has got in store for me for the next couple of hours, any guilt has well and truly passed. What's that old saying about making hay while the sun's shining?

Sometimes these screenings are held in the big public cinemas around Central London, but just as often they're in private screening rooms. These mini movie houses are invisible to the public eye, but they're everywhere. Take a walk around Soho – one of London's most colourful areas and home to many of the outlets that I freelance for. If you look up you'll probably spot prostitutes in their top floor apartments, but look down and there will be a plethora of private basement cinemas. Thankfully I know a lot more about the latter than the former. These screening rooms, mainly owned by film companies and production houses, are all too easy to get used to. Want a big comfy chair to curl up in? You got it. Extra leg room? That too. And have I mentioned the free food and drink provided?

It's not all good, though. For example, on some very rare occasions (i.e. when someone else is paying) I've enjoyed other benefits such as First Class air travel. It is great – until I have to pay for a flight myself and can only afford Economy. You see, once you've turned left on a 747, going in the other direction just isn't the same again. It's similar with these private screenings. They spoil you. I've got so used to the nibbles, wine and lack of adverts now, that a Saturday-night trip to the Odeon just doesn't feel quite the same as it used to. I always maintain that one of the most important things about being a showbiz reporter is to remember what your audience wants. How do they live? What excites them? But when you're being plied with exclusive film showings and all-you-can-drink Chablis, you realise your experience has moved a long way away from the norm. So it's important to keep two feet on the ground, even if those feet are currently stretching out on to the shagpile of a luxurious private cinema.

As much as this has become a normal part of my life, the people I watch these films with aren't always the same folk. In fact, the audiences differ enormously. Ideally I'll be with other reporters like myself, all of us anxious as to what the movie star we're about to watch, and later interview, will be like. While we're all hoping to get the scoop and we certainly keep our cards close to our chests when it comes to chatting about what we're going to ask, there's no real rivalry. As much as I believe in the importance of the entertainment world, we know we're not doing brain surgery. What's the point in getting too competitive?

That's not an opinion shared by the second type of audience I often watch movies with – the film critic. Wow, those guys like one-upmanship. As I sit waiting for the curtains to open and the show to start, I can hear them sat behind me, trying to outdo each other:

'Yeah, Warner Brothers has invited me to a special screening of Film X next week.'

'Oh, I've seen that already. Scorsese put on a screening for me last month.'

Whatever.

I don't think film critics really like us reporters. In their eyes, we're not proper film fans. It may be true that we're not as nerdily obsessive as them, and as we're mainly young women and they're old men, I suspect they're a bit intimidated too, but as I always say, showbiz should be fun. If we reporters laugh, gossip and enjoy ourselves I don't think that's a bad thing. When you're in a cinema full of film critics it sometimes seems like they actually want to hate the film, solely so they can vent some spleen and make some bad jokes in their review. Anger appears to be their default setting.

But then, even I get angry with the third type of audience – the liggers. What's a ligger, you ask? A ligger is someone who has no real reason to be at a swanky event, but who hoovers up the free finger food, having somehow wangled an invite anyway. At some of the bigger preview screenings in the evenings, it can seem that the whole world and his wife are on the guest list. I swear that one time back in my office days, the drippy guy who worked in the post room came up to me and asked what I'd thought of the film last night. I hadn't been invited, I told him. But somehow he had. With liggers, it's all about whom you can sweet talk into putting you on the guest list. He then went on to give me a detailed review and recommended me trying to see it. I bit my tongue and tried to stay calm.

It's in these more packed screenings that you see all sorts – media boys with their man bags and cool trainers, probably from some marketing department somewhere; imposing girls from advertising companies, tottering around in their designer heels; and bleary-eyed bloggers who only leave their bedrooms for the offer of a free movie and sandwich. So is it wrong to get annoyed when you're fighting for seats with people who don't even properly work in the industry? Am I turning into one of those miserable old critics by complaining? Probably. It's at these moments that I once again need to keep my feet on the ground and remember what I've got and, more importantly, what I could very easily *not* have.

The film over – no trailers, no people talking, no teenagers on their mobile phones – and with my name ticked off on the posh PR girl's list, I'm now ready to do the interview. In my job, I'm not really supposed to have an opinion on whether the movie's any good or not; it's just about getting the story. Does it matter for my article if the film's a real stinker? Not really. It might, of course, annoy me if I'd paid £15 to see it at my local cinema, but as I've just spent the last two hours with a glass of wine, a comfy chair and hot guy on the big screen *all for free*, I'm not bothered one bit . . .

Who wouldn't have sleepless nights worrying that, one day, all of that could so easily be taken away?

Tom Hanks

There's no other way to say it – Tom Hanks is just so bloody nice. I suppose when you've had such a successful film career, with nothing really left to prove, then there's no major reason to be in a bad mood (not that it doesn't stop some stars – see the chapter 'Harrison Ford' coming up). With Tom, though, it's not just that he's achieved everything he could ever have dreamt of. It's more as if he's just got niceness in his DNA. From the moment that you walk into the interview room to the moment that you close the door on the way out, he's charm personified – funny, smart, engaging. He uses your name, he looks you in the eye, he answers your questions. All of those things might, I admit, just sound like common-sense politeness but you'd be surprised just how many celebrities can't seem to manage such a small thing. Chatting with Tom Hanks, on the other hand, isn't like talking to an untouchable, double Oscar-winning star of movie blockbusters such as *Forrest Gump*, *The Da Vinci Code* and the *Toy Story* movies. It's more like you're just having a gossip with your best pal.

Aside from genetics, I also credit a lot of his likeability to hard work. Tom Hanks was not an overnight success or a spoilt brat child star. After growing up a self-confessed theatre geek, then some ropey TV work as a young man, he had to plough through several years of graft in fun-but-flimsy films. Some were hits, some flops and it took a good while before he started to be taken seriously as an actor, not least by himself (Tom thinks his performances only really came of age in the early nineties). It's easy to think of him now as a legend but he had to *earn* those stripes over a long period. With that kind of slog behind you, it must be a lot easier to be considerate and fair.

While I've never heard anyone say 'Tom Hanks? I can't bloody stand him!', I do think that guys could give him a bit more respect. He has so much to teach them. Consider the evidence for a second, gentlemen: Tom Hanks is in one of the best-loved romantic movies of all time, *Sleepless in Seattle*. Prior to that, he'd been mainly known for some fairly broad comedies. In *Sleepless*, though, that sweet jokiness he'd found fame with was transformed into something romantic and tender. Suddenly it was an asset that could win over the girl, something gently sexy. Tom might not ever have had a physique like Daniel Craig, but I know which one would be nicer to have a laugh with at the top of the Empire State Building. Boys in the gym, take note.

Long marriages are a rarity in showbiz, even more so when both partners are actors, but Tom's relationship with Rita Wilson has lasted 25 years, including several years working together as producers of films such as *My Big Fat Greek Wedding*. Having met Tom Hanks a few times now, I can understand why. *I* wouldn't want to ever leave him either. The fact that Tom is Hollywood's most successful ever movie star, with box office receipts of over $8 billion around the world, shows that sometimes – thankfully – the nice guys do win.

Demands

It's true – some hard-nosed celebrities do ask for weird stuff. I suppose when you know you've got power, you just want to try it out and see how far you can push things. Most, certainly, defy logic. Unfortunately it's usually down to the entourage, educated people who frankly could do a lot better than pretend that the sun shines out of their client's backside, to run around after them.

These teams – assistants, publicists, stylists etc. – try to behave like robots around us in the press, so as to give off the impression that everything in their client's world is perfect and harmonious, 24/7. But deep down even the most steely publicist is only human; the façade can't stay up for ever. This is where my being friendly with everyone really pays off. Sometimes a member of the entourage gets asked to do such ridiculous things that all they want after a hard day's bowing and scraping is to cry into a glass of Sauvignon Blanc and unload their gripes on to me. I'm fine with that. I'll be an agony aunt if needed.

Do they know that, by sharing them with me, their stories might one day end up in print? Of course. While they could never publicly slate their client (they'd never work again if they did), who's to say they can't 'accidentally' reveal a story over a few drinks in the bar? The result? The satisfaction of knowing that their bitchy truths will be spread around the world while at the same time being somewhat distanced from the finger of blame. If you're a star reading this, the message is hopefully clear: be nice to your team. They're just as good at revealing the horrid truth about you as they are at making your lemon-infused tea.

Everyone likes revenge, even nobodies.

Hence stories of demanding behaviour are constantly coming my way from industry insiders at the end of their tether. For example:

There's the famous big-lunged starlet who demanded five of her people accompany her to the toilet at a TV studio. Either she's got some serious fear of loneliness or she just likes to test how far her entourage will go. Sorry love, but one of them's had enough of having to stand around outside the cubicle waiting for you to finish your business.

Equally precious is the camp British acting hunk who dramatically proclaimed that he would only have a certain, exclusive type of make-up on his delicate skin, one that needed to be shipped over from Paris (obviously). He probably wouldn't have noticed the difference if his groomer had just slapped on the Max Factor and kept quiet, but still, panicked assistants spent a fortune on shipping over the foundation to keep him happy. When he didn't even thank anyone for all their effort, one of them couldn't keep quiet any longer.

We've all heard, I'm sure, the whispers about a certain star demanding her hotel suite to be redecorated white and scattered with similarly pale floral displays and expensive scented candles before she'd do any interviews. Well, it's more than just idle gossip. A colleague actually saw the room in question. She was in there interviewing the star, trying to focus on getting a good story while battling blindness from the sea of alabaster all around her, struggling not to choke from the heady perfume spewing from three hundred quid's worth of Diptyques. That night, after a stressful couple of days working with the prissy diva, one of the event organisers couldn't wait to plonk herself down in a bar with me and my friend and get it all off her chest.

It can't be fun being the flunky under orders to carry out such a hasty makeover but future PR girls should be aware that it can be even worse. Addicts are hell to work with, and a lot more common in the celebrity world than you might expect. If you ever see someone famous constantly sipping from a glass of water while they're being interviewed, don't take it for granted that it's the finest bottled H_2O they're enjoying. I discovered that one household name's 'water' was actually neat vodka, constantly topped up by an assistant during his day of interviews, his answers no doubt become more and more incoherent as the hours passed. Spare a thought too for the aide sent out on to the streets of Rome to find cocaine for a major movie star, only to come back with what would technically be described as 'bad shit'. Not that the star realised this until he'd shovelled mountains of it up his nose and made himself ill, forcing him to spend the next day of press interviews frequently running to the toilet to throw up. 'He's got a bug,' we were told by a concerned publicist. Yeah right. That famous bug you get when you've snorted half a pack of Persil up your nostrils.

Often though, demands I hear about are just more time-consuming and boring than illegal or illicit. Take the case of the legendary Hollywood actor who, when staying in a London hotel with his small daughter, demanded that she be shielded from anything that might make her realise that Dad was seriously famous. So it was that a publicist whose job was normally to make sure the talent was as visible as possible, now had to hourly comb the hotel for magazines, newspapers and TV channels that could give away this fella's fame to his sensitive littl'un. Not easy when the actor in question was in town solely to promote his new movie and was basically *everywhere*. Fame, we know, can reward you with many beautiful things. Paranoia, however, is one of the less attractive.

Harrison Ford

My older brother couldn't believe it when I told him I'd be meeting the man who wasn't just Indiana Jones but also Han Solo. To be honest, I'd always been more excited by the former than the latter. When my bro put on his *Star Wars* videos every Sunday morning as a child, I used to sullenly lope off to my bedroom. The one time I did watch one of the films with him, I asked so many questions ('Why is it called a light *saver*?') that he made me promise never to bother him again. My interest in spaceships and aliens has been negligible ever since.

But as Indiana, Harrison was something else. I loved the way that he transformed from gentle archaeology professor Henry Jones into bull whipping action man Indy when the scent of adventure got to him. He seemed to be the best of both worlds; the boffin that needed to be looked after by a kindly woman, and the tough guy who'd protect you from the Nazis. If I was too young to really understand all this at the time I certainly knew that I had a childhood crush on Harrison. I had similarly innocent feelings about my friend Heidi's father, but all he could offer were bad dad jokes and a baseball cap he wore when he was doing the gardening. Harrison had laconic quips and a fedora. No competition. And now I was off to meet him . . . *in Italy*.

It's dawn and I'm rubbing my eyes on the Heathrow Express. The man sat opposite me tries to stifle a yawn but ends up with a pained expression more silly than if he'd just let it out in the first place. I take another sip of my latte but frankly, nothing's going to wake me up. That's the problem with work trips to the Continent: film and record companies figure that most of it is close enough for us to do a return trip in a day. True enough I suppose, and it obviously saves on hotel expenses. But even getting excited about a Harrison Ford interview is difficult if you have to get up at 4 a.m.

After the tasty English breakfast I devour at the terminal – not to mention the disgusting, congealed one on the aeroplane – I'm a little more fired up by the time I reach Venice and water taxi my way over to the stylish hotel. The flight has been spent writing out questions, mainly fluffy stuff but a few more filmy ones than I would usually ask. It's not every day you meet someone whose work represents happy childhood memories for so many people. My brother used to play with this man every day (well, his *Star Wars* action figure). The Italian hospitality couldn't be better either – pizza slices, cured meats and olives on tap in the hotel waiting room – and sitting with the Adriatic sun streaming through the open window certainly makes a pleasant change from grimy London. Despite the early start I begin to feel that actually, I couldn't be happier. I'm getting Indiana Jones and a tan all in the same day.

'Holly Forrest, from the UK?'

I'm called into the interview room and I prepare myself to come face to face with a legend. Unfortunately, when I head in, that legend looks as if he'd rather be anywhere than here. Sunshine and olives obviously don't hold the same appeal to Harrison as they do to me. He's sat down and looking nervous, something that immediately unnerves me too. I'm trying to stay smiley and confident by keeping eye contact, but suddenly all I can focus on is his left ear. It's hypnotic – there, lodged in his lobe and twinkling proudly in the Venetian sunshine, is an earring. I can't believe it. The only jewels that Indiana Jones should be interested in are mythical treasure troves and ancient relics. Then I remember that I'd seen a few stories about the offending accessory in the papers recently, most people aghast that a man in his sixties, famed for playing no-nonsense tough guys, would fancy a trip to Claire's Accessories to get blinged up. A new relationship with Calista Flockhart, 22 years his junior, was obviously having an effect. The earring isn't even that big but the more I try to not look at it, the more I stare. I'm like a moth to a flame.

Finally I tear myself away and concentrate on shaking the great man's hand. Harrison is a man who certainly suits his years. Lines might have aged his face but, earring aside, he still looks great; weathered but sexy. I'm momentarily transported back to being nine years old again and I've beaten my brother in the battle for the video player. He wants to watch *Return of the Jedi* but I get there first with *Raiders of the Lost Ark*. Result.

'So, Harrison, lovely to meet you. You're a hero to so many of our readers, all of whom love to watch your films in their free time. I'm just wondering though – what do you like to do when you're not saving the day?'

A pleasant enough question, I think. A nice little ice-breaker. If only . . .

'Well,' Harrison growls, like a bear waking up, 'if you'd done your research . . . you'd know that I trained as a carpenter and now spend a lot of time on my ranch.'

That made sense. The man in front of me certainly looked as if he'd be happier with a saw in his hands or covered in engine oil. He is glaring at me, stony faced. You know how I just thought how attractive he still is? Well now I'm thinking that the very same face is actually pretty scary and intimidating. A shiver runs down my spine and I look away from his stare, only managing to go as far as that bloody earring again.

Hopefully you've read enough about my life now to believe me when I say that I don't think anyone is unpleasant without reason. Maybe it's the people around them who turn people nasty? Or an issue from childhood? Whatever, I'll always try to give a bad interviewee the benefit of the doubt (even while secretly cursing how difficult it will be to write a vaguely interesting thousand-word article about them). In Harrison's case, maybe is it just because he's done so many interviews in his time that he can't be bothered to pretend any more? He was actually right – I hadn't researched the answer to that particular question. But when it's such an innocuous query, who would? It was like trying to elicit a conversation out of a gruff car mechanic when all he wants to be doing is lying under your engine, tinkering with your exhaust.

Colleagues who've also met Harrison say exactly the same thing. I've got no reason to believe that he's a particularly horrible man; he just seems to be someone who makes major Hollywood films despite hating everything that goes with the territory. *Especially* the press. I carry on the interview with a set of the most harmless questions imaginable, desperate not to get barked at again. The answers are begrudgingly – though thankfully not angrily – given. Playing it safe might mean that I don't get my feelings hurt again, but it also means that I leave Italy without a hint of any exciting material. Back in rainy London I find myself quickly missing the balmy continental weather and the tasty pizza. I certainly don't miss Harrison, though.

I don't have the heart to call up my brother and tell him what our childhood hero has been like with me. In fact, I tried to never think about it again, until now. Moaning about an uncooperative celebrity can be fun sometimes, but I'd much rather try to keep my treasured memories precious. Memories where Harrison is still the dashing Indiana Jones, saving the day on an exciting crusade; whip on his belt, fedora on his head and definitely *no* earring.

Tom Cruise

'Bollocks!'

'Erica Louise Richards, I'm telling you, it's true!'

'It's bollocks, Holly!'

'It's not. You're the prime example.'

'Still bollocks.'

'It's not. You just can't admit your true feelings, that's all. I'll say again: at least half of the women that say they don't fancy Tom Cruise actually *do*. It's just not deemed cool to admit it, what with all his kinda weird behaviour and everything. But seriously, most women I know would jump at the chance, whatever they claim. I'll happily admit it. I'm not embarrassed. I would *ruin* him.'

We burst into laughter and any pretence that we're actually watching *Vanilla Sky* on the TV, let alone understanding what the hell the plot is about, goes out of the window. Still, even in our wine-fuelled playfulness I like to think that I've raised an interesting point. Mention Tom's name and most people think of the same things: intriguing relationships, Scientology, jumping up and down on Oprah's sofa. Here's a guy who had the perfect image for so long (when no one would be ashamed of saying they lusted after him), but whose questionable moves in the last ten years have completely changed how he's perceived. It's a shame I think.

Whatever is going on in Tom's head, on screen he still exudes the kind of movie star charisma most actors can only dream of. Despite what Erica reckons, that's undeniably sexy. So while his name sets off certain thoughts for some people, whenever I hear it I think first about Tom the fearless, feisty and (here we go) fit leading man.

'I'm gonna tell him how he can be cool again,' I slur to Erica, slamming down my wine glass on the coffee table with the confidence of someone who's just had a lightbulb moment.

'What? You interviewing him soon then?'

She has a good point. My boozy logic has forgotten that very few journalists ever get close to the man. If I'd been doing this job in the eighties maybe I'd have got my chance but certainly in my time Tom has limited himself to his infamous premiere walkabouts rather than actual sit-down, one-to-one interviews. I guess he just got fed-up with journalists banging on about religion and rumours and he was powerful enough to say 'No more.' Only interviewers as famous as Tom himself – Oprah, etc. – get to really probe the man these days . . .

'Er . . . Well, no. I'm not actually interviewing him. But I'm gonna . . . I'm gonna . . . I'm gonna . . . WRITE HIM A LETTER!'

You know how, when you're drunk, you come up with ideas that in that moment feel up there with the wheel, the internet and waterproof mascara in terms of amazingness. This was one of those times. I open up my laptop and Erica squashes up beside me on the sofa.

'A letter!' she squeals, clapping her hands. 'Rocking it old-skool!'

I open up a blank Word page on the screen.

'Right then,' I say. 'Forget L. Ron Cupboard or whatever he's called. It's me that should be Tom's adviser.'

I start typing recklessly faster than *Top Gun*'s Maverick in his -14. Here, shamefully, is what I wrote:

Dear Mr Cruise,

I hope you don't mind me writing to you but I'm a big fan and there are a couple of things I'd like to say to you. You see I've been having an argument with my ~~slutty~~ perfect housemate, Erica, the main point of which is about whether people still fancy you or not. She claims she doesn't any more and that for her it's all about Channing Tatum these days but how can you find someone sexy who's got not one but two girl's names, FFS? Anyway, I'm rambling and Erica is punching me on the arm.

The thing is, Tommy – can I call you Tommy? – I want everyone to think you're cool and sexy again. I grew up with you and your smile and 'You can't handle the truth' and 'Show me the money!' and all that stuff. Let's get that back shall we? Let's make everyone proud to say they love you again.

So here's what you have to do: get back to basics, Tommo – can I call you Tommo? What I mean is, it might be time to act normal again.

All that 'Cruise Control' stuff, where people can't even look you in the eye? And all those lawyers? Enough already. Seriously, whenever I'm asked to write something about you, especially if it mentions your love life or religion, my editor goes into overdrive with patronising warnings about being careful and not getting sued. I mean, Jesus Christ . . . (Oh sorry, I know you're a Scientologist – but I'm sure you'll have heard of him.)

Okay, so you're just a guy wanting to defend himself against lies. I appreciate it's not nice being lied about. There was this miserable cow where I worked once – Nicola from Accounts – who claimed that I'd slept with this guy Oscar, our publisher's assistant. Not true. Complete and utter lies. Okay, we had a snog at the Christmas party. Okay, I went back to his place. Okay, I stayed over and had to do the 'walk of shame' the next day at work when I came in wearing the same clothes I had on at the party. But I didn't sleep with him. And I made sure Nicola knew. So I can understand that you're just protecting yourself but the thing is T – can I call you T? – **the less weird you act, the less us journos will hunt around for juicy stuff to write about you.** I've even put that bit in bold to show you how important it is. Oh hang on. Aren't you dyslexic? Can you even read this? Well anyway, that's the equation. Cool films minus the weird behaviour = a Tom that everyone loves again. You might even bag your own Oscar, ha ha ha! (I can write scripts you know, if you ever need any.)

While I've got you here, Tom, can I just mention something else too, please? You know your legendary two-hour walkabouts at film premieres? Any chance of just cutting them down a bit?

The thing is, if I'm on a Tom Cruise red carpet, of course I have to wait for you to say something into my microphone. I can hardly say to an editor 'Soz but I left before Tom got to me . . . but I did get a few words with Caprice if that's any good?' But can't you just . . . hurry things along a little? Luckily the *War of the Worlds* premiere – when you first did that whole 'chatting to a fan's mum on a mobile' thing – was held in the summer so although my feet ached from standing around for ages, at least I wasn't shivering. That last *Mission: Impossible* movie though? It was in the middle of freakin' December! It was so cold even you were wearing a dad-jumper underneath your suit (not a good look, btw. If you need a stylist I've got a good friend called Daisy who's very discreet). Frankly, when I'm battling frostbite it's tough to care about you, Tom, however sexy I find you. I'm stood there for hours chilling my butt off simply because you're spending hours having snaps taken with a load of tourists. Not good. I love you but even I laughed at that time you got sprayed with water by a fake micro-phone. It just broke up the long wait a bit. I know working the red carpet is your 'thing'. But getting home in time to put my feet up and watch *Keeping Up with the Kardashians* is mine, so maybe there's a middle ground?

Or, just have all your premieres in July?

Love from Holly x

PS. Say hi to Suri for me.

Erica is curled up into a ball, sleeping like a baby. Suddenly it's all I want to do too. So I save the letter to a folder marked 'Work in Progress', tell myself that 'Tom Cruise, Hollywood' should be enough of an address for the envelope . . . and shut my eyes.

'I'll print it out tomorrow,' I mumble, half asleep.

Thankfully, I never do.

Rappers

In more than 15 years as a showbiz reporter, I've only ever walked out of one interview – and that was before it had even started. It was for a female hip-hop star. Frankly, I just couldn't wait for her any longer. This was back in the day when I still worked full-time for the magazine and couldn't just block out hours of my day to hold on for an ageing R'n'B diva. 'She runs on hip-hop time I'm afraid,' I was told by the posh publicist, a girl so gentrified just the very word 'hip-hop' seemed weird coming out of her mouth. Two hours later, still nothing had happened. Hip-hop time, it appeared, was some kind of scientific anomaly, unlike the seconds, minutes and hours that we know. This timescale was more fluid, looser. In short it meant this star would turn up when she wanted to and the floating minions around her were too scared to try to chivvy her along.

As any juicy content from my interview with her would only have been used in a small gossip column I was writing – and which I had to get on with fast – I took an executive decision . . . and walked. 'I'm sorry but I just don't have the time for this. I'm going,' I announced as I marched out of the hotel suite. Unprofessional maybe, but then keeping journalists waiting for a couple of hours isn't exactly the height of professionalism. The publicity team looked shocked. Essentially they just expect us to do what we're told, like a herd of unquestioning animals. That day, however, I didn't have the time to be a lemming. As I walked down the corridor and past the room in which she was holed up I heard a lot of shouting and laughing, a real riot. It's as if she wanted us to hear how great a time she was having while we had to sit and twiddle our thumbs. I doubt she had a serious reason to delay the interviews for that long. It was all posturing. She was the 'boss' and we just had to do what she wanted.

Except I didn't. Walking down the road on my way back to work I felt no guilt. In fact, I felt liberated.

Posturing is, of course, a massive part of hip-hop culture. Interestingly, though, it can manifest itself in other ways as well. With many urban artists, their posturing actually involves being extremely quiet and introverted, like they're almost too scared to talk. In fact, I've often found myself *wishing* for the kind of brassy, noisy behaviour I heard coming from Miss X's room that day, since so many hip-hop stars that I've met since have been so boringly meek and mild in an interview situation, despite being so aggressive on record. Silence is as much an attitude as shoutiness.

So when you go to interview a rapper you never know which side you're going to get from them – the loud but late one or the on-time but tacit one? In an ideal world there'd be middle-ground – noisy *and* on-time – but I guess there's just not enough attitude in that.

There is, however, one thing you can *always* rely on: whether late or punctual, shouty or mute, these guys and girls like to surround themselves with a massive entourage. They're an essential part of the image.

I remember one rapper I interviewed had at least half a dozen of the biggest bruisers you can imagine in the room with him, all wearing matching basketball vests. None of them spoke. They just looked annoyed and tapped away on their mobiles as I did the interview. Who were they? What were their jobs? Had the star himself been a chatty, fun-loving extrovert then I might have asked him but alas he was putting on an act like so many before him: quiet, mumbly, a little bit dull. I was getting serious mixed messages: on the one hand, this guy was all attitude, on the other, he was as fragile as a church mouse. It reminded me of being in school, where there was always some kid who was really mouthy and cocky at school, but who would go home every night and be a real mummy's boy. Watch Eminem in his semi-autobiographical film *8 Mile* and that's pretty much the case.

Rappers often say that their split personality is down to the fact that they're just like actors, their on-stage attitude more of a performance than anything real – Eminem's angry Slim Shady character is a great example. If that's true then some of these guys are as chameleon-like a performer as De Niro. Give them all Oscars. You see, if you actually met 50 Cent, for example, you'd be hard pushed to find someone less likely to take you to the 'candy shop' to let you lick his 'lollipop'. The real Curtis Jackson acted so withdrawn when I met him he seemed like more of an antiques fair kind of guy.

The day after I had got bored with waiting for the hip-hop diva and walked, I asked a more patient reporter how things had gone:

'She had a huge entourage in the room, looking miserable. And her answers were quiet, polite and just a bit boring really. Not like how I'd expected.'

No surprise there then. And by walking out I had managed to get back to the office at a decent time, finish my piece, and then head home to spend the evening with my flatmate. A much healthier way of living than wasting your time waiting for a stuck-up madam.

Over dinner that night I put on some of her songs. Erica and I still rapped along like maniacs (well, I kind of 'talked/shouted' in that way that only middle-class white girls attempting to be street can), throwing shapes with our hands in between mouthfuls of shepherd's pie. This is how I like my hip-hop, I realised: on an album. Split personalities are so much easier to deal with when they're safely lodged in your iPod.

Obituaries

Think of a celebrity over the age of 80 and the chances are their obituary has already been written. Sound macabre? Maybe a little. But macabre is nothing compared to the feeling of being caught out when an old-timer shuffles off and your boss is shouting at you for some copy to go on the website. Prepare early and your life (not to mention their death) becomes a lot easier.

That's not to say it's always easy. While freelancing for an agency once, gathering material for all the radio stations that subscribed to the service, a colleague asked me to check their store of obits. While largely that involved me going into the relevant folder on the computer and making sure the scripts were still correct and up-to-date, I also needed to write a few new ones. After all, a star who was firing on all cylinders the last time these guys did an obit check might now be knockin' on heaven's door. I had to ensure that, should the worst happen, the agency was ready to send out an obit to their hundreds of subscribers within seconds of these creaky legends breathing their last. *The Times* might like to finely craft their detailed obituaries column over several days, the epic result appearing a week or so after the death, and invariably proving a fine read. But The Beach 96.3 (The Best Mix of the 80s, 90s & Today!) isn't quite so patient. It needed to have everything ready to go, enabling listeners to almost immediately enjoy a 30-second summary of a famous person's life, in between the latest local news and the new single from Maroon 5.

I had a quick think about which icons had been looking a bit pasty recently or living a bit close to the edge, and wrote some new scripts to have in store should the worst happen. The problem was, as much as I wished it wasn't so, I knew that my words alone just wouldn't be enough. In our celebrity-driven world, we don't just want to hear a journalist's thoughts on the amazing life of a recently departed, much-loved superstar, we want to hear what other celebrities think too. Calling a star up when the news breaks is one option, but if they're a close friend, they'll probably be too upset to talk. This method also uses up valuable time, time that your competitors might already have used to send out their own obituaries to their own subscribers. The result? You lose the race. However, if you record a few celebs reminiscing about their old pal and expressing their condolences *in advance*, then all you have to do when Grandma or Grandad X finally heads towards the spirit world is hit 'send' and the job's done. It's all in the planning. (If you think this sounds flippant, then I agree. Believe me though, this is the kind of attitude that drives a newsroom and I'm just trying to paint a picture. I don't think anything can prepare you for the ruthlessness of the news environment. I've even seen hard-hitting news journalists taking bets on what a serial killer's final tally will be.)

The question is, how do you call a celeb in your contacts book and ask them if they could pre-record their feelings about someone dying that hasn't actually died yet? They certainly never teach you *that* at college. The answer, as it is so often in journalism, is simply to grow a thick skin. You know how you convince yourself that a doctor won't bat an eyelid at your embarrassing medical problem because they've seen it all before and have become blasé about such things? Journos are the same. What VDs are to GPs, awkward situations are to reporters. Experience has taught me that you just have to get on with it and don't think too much. More surprising, perhaps, is that a lot of the celebs I called on that day didn't think too much about it either; they just did it. Sure, some people politely declined. On the whole, though, people in the media know how these things work. They understand the game. If your voice is going to be heard by millions across the country, expressing sadness at the loss of a great friend and entertainer, why not play your part when you're coherent and sharp rather than when you're in pieces and genuinely mourning their loss? One guy was so prepared to talk about his lifelong work colleague, now in ailing health, that he even demanded to be paid for it. I didn't know whether to be mightily offended at his insensitivity or, with my freelance journalist's hat on, to admire his chutzpah.

Still, nothing can prepare you for a shock celebrity death. If you'd have asked me on 21 January 2008 which megastar I expected to leave us soon, Heath Ledger would have been the last name on my list. Some young stars you can prepare for, knowing that their escalating drug habit or scary weight loss is a worrying sign of something critical. But there were no indications with Heath. Twenty-four hours later I was hurriedly writing his obituary for a website. While many people might have achieved more in the entertainment world than him, his death affected me because his films were part of my life – and, arguably, his best performances were still ahead of us all. This wasn't someone from another era, an icon of the past whom I only thought of as elderly and frail. Here was a man around my age whose movies I had grown up with. When River Phoenix and Kurt Cobain died young in the nineties of course I was affected but that was long before I was working as a professional journalist. Now I was faced with having to do a job at the same time as fighting a lump in my throat. Not easy. With nothing planned in advance – who was expecting a 28-year-old to die? – I found myself writing from scratch. The more I learnt, the more difficult it became. The important dates in his life were not from way before I was born. No, here was someone for whom things were all so recent. Success, marriage, fatherhood – they'd all occurred in the last ten years. I posted the piece as quickly as possible, complete with a host of thoughts from various celebs' Twitter and Facebook accounts. At least I wouldn't have to make any phone calls. For although my skin has been toughened by years of London media life – a necessity in this job – sometimes you can only take so much. I'm not a complete robot.

After shutting down my computer, I burst uncontrollably into tears. I was crying mainly for the loss of such a young talent, a man whom I had loved in several films and whom I had inter-viewed on a couple of occasions and found sweet and charming (despite an obvious discomfort with fame). But I was also crying partly with relief, strangely thankful that I felt genuinely saddened by the loss. It was proof that, after all these years, I was still human.

Hugh Jackman

One unremarkable day in 1998, I made my way into London's West End to meet a star of the stage musical *Oklahoma!* I had no idea who he was, but I'd been won over by a publicist's pitch that he was 'on the brink of success'. I hear this claim quite often, but since I fancied an afternoon out of the office I took a risk on meeting this so-called Next Big Thing, even though there was a good chance he might never actually find fame. I'm *so* glad that I did, since the guy in question went on to become one of Hollywood's biggest stars: Hugh Jackman.

One of the great things about Mr Jackman is that *he* never seems to change, even as his fame explodes around him. That's certainly not always the case with celebrities. If you meet a star several times over the years, it can be easy to notice them morphing from one thing into another, and it can be quite scary. Take one British starlet I encountered over the years. She began life as the down-to-earth girl next door and my first meeting with her was just like two old mates having a chat. I was there primarily to discuss her beauty routine for a feature I was writing and she proceeded to debunk all the latest gimmicks and expensive potions with a funny cynicism that made great copy. 'I can't do a bloody thing with my thatch,' she laughed, pointing to her messy hair.

'What's the point in spending loads of money on products that won't work?!'

By the next time we met, Hollywood had beckoned (very successfully too) and while she wasn't unpleasant, the barriers were certainly starting to come up. Her grooming was just a little bit neater, her answers that teeny bit more guarded. The atmosphere felt less like 'old friends meeting up', and more like a job interview. But on the third time, she refused to even sit up when talking to me, instead reclining on the plush hotel sofa like Cleopatra, constantly sighing in an exaggerated way and playing with her now long and lustrous LA bouffant.

Success can so easily go to your head – and, it seems, to your hair.

Luckily not everyone succumbs. Some people – maybe because of how they were brought up or perhaps because of the people around them – stay happily relaxed no matter how much bigger their name has become on movie posters. Meeting those people is always a relief. When they also happen to be as dashing and as sweet as Hugh Jackman, then it's time for a double celebration.

Perhaps Hugh has his Aussie background to owe for his inherent appeal? The Antipodeans, of course, have a huge presence in global entertainment, from Kylie to Kidman, Crowe to Crocodile Dundee. Many are megastars, lauded with awards, adulation and, in the case of Russell, the odd court case, but interview any of them on the red carpet and there remains a lovable earthiness in their responses that's a million miles away from LA swagger. I mean, can you imagine Taylor Lautner saying: 'Bloody hell, mate. This is a ripper, ain't it? I'm done up like a show pony here!'?

Hugh also found fame internationally relatively late in life. He was in his early thirties when we all fell for his hairy Wolverine (if you'll excuse the expression), and I'm convinced that this can make a big difference to a celebrity's attitude. If you grow up with success from childhood, it's easy to feel that you're entitled to it. On the other hand, slog away in theatre and daytime telly for years and when stardom does come you don't take it for granted.

Unknown he may have been when I first met him, but even then Hugh's laidback banter was a blessed relief after endless megastar snobbery. Over the years Hugh's willingness to promote his films, his continued friendliness during interviews and, crucially, the fact that he doesn't seem to have changed since that day when I spoke to him, means that he's always a pleasure to meet. Even in the crazy throng of a premiere he still somehow remembers that I took a chance on him when he was a no one and thanks me for it (I've never told him how that first interview actually ended up as little more than a few lines). He's hosted the Oscars, sung on Broadway and snogged Halle Berry, but he still seems as much in awe of all that as we are. That's very appealing. On the face of things he's blossomed into one of Hollywood's most sophisticated leading men, but thankfully, down under, he's still . . . Down Under.

Smells

A couple of years ago, I smelt like Victoria Beckham. Then for a bit my whiff was unmistakably Leona Lewis. Now, apparently, I exude Beyoncé.

However, while I confess to being a celebrity fragrance anorak – a lot of them, in my defence, being given to me for free – I do realise that simply by dousing myself in the scent of citrus, wood and apple martini doesn't turn me into Sarah Jessica Parker. That is just the marketing ploy. Buy a celeb fragrance and you're supposed to think you're tapping into part of an A-Lister's very soul, gradually morphing into your showbiz icon with every spray. That's the power of endorsements. Unfortunately, though, merely squirting on a bit of Kylie's 'Couture' doesn't give me her bank-balance, boyfriend or bottom. Luckily I quite like the smell (musk stripes, vanilla sorbet and white cedar, apparently). Even the boys have got in on the game, with everyone from P Diddy to Peter Andre flogging off their pheromones.

Old-time Hollywood legend Elizabeth Taylor began the celebrity fragrance craze back in the eighties, but for a long while the perfumes were expensive and exclusive, the famous not wanting to water down their aura by selling out from the shelves of Superdrug. However, the amount of money that Jennifer Lopez made in her first year on the perfume mass market soon changed other stars' minds (her 'Glow' was America's second biggest selling fragrance when launched in 2002). Now you can pick up some celeb scents for the price of a couple of drinks.

Do I believe that Jenny Lopez was actually sat in her apron at her kitchen table mixing scents long into the night, personally coming up with just the pong that she thought exactly represented 'brand J-Lo'? Of course not. Again, it's all part of the illusion. Naturally, I don't think any star would sign off a fragrance without checking the smell themselves, but ultimately these scents are mainly manufactured by the same two or three big beauty companies. Rihanna, Paris Hilton and Jessica Simpson might all compete to outsell each other in the Duty Frees of the world, but look at the small print on the back of the perfume boxes and they're all made by the same people.

Trying to get some decent journalism out of this showbiz trend isn't the easiest thing in the world. There are often glamorous launches for these products where the star 'creator' turns up looking pretty and has her photo taken holding the bottle in front of a heavily branded backdrop. Then there'll be a press conference where she tries in vain to make describing a smell vaguely interesting ('I wanted to capture the magic of a first kiss, a setting sun, the tingle of champagne on your tongue,' etc.). A wealth of journalists will be there wondering exactly how we can turn this puff into an article while simultaneously worrying whether we'll be able to fit yet another bottle of celeb smelly on the bathroom shelf. In a notoriously superficial industry, these kinds of launches are perhaps the shallowest of all. Yet the power of celebrity is such that journalists are simply too scared to miss one, *just in case* the superstar says something exciting. Not to mention that the perfume manufacturers also happen to be regular advertisers in our mags and no editor wants to bite the hand that feeds.

I've been known to try to alleviate my boredom at such events, by making up my own list of celebrity aromas; as the famous person a few feet in front of me waffles on about 'top notes of Spanish jasmine, reminiscent of the thrill of a holiday romance and the passion of a Mediterranean breeze', I try to describe what these perfumes *should* smell like:

Christina Aguilera. The blurb says: 'notes of fruit sorbet, black-currant tea, and a sillage of musk and vanilla'.

What it should smell like: 'a hint of latex and fake tan delicately combined with last night's KFC'.

Britney Spears. The blurb says: 'a fruity mix of lychee, golden quince and kiwi'.

What it should smell like: 'essence of fag ash, bubblegum and baby's nappies'.

Madonna. The blurb says: 'notes of gardenia, creamy tuberose and neroli'.

What it should smell like: 'the unmistakable stench of three hours in the gym'.

Mariah Carey. The blurb says: 'gentle cherry blossom and wild berries'.

What it should smell like: '100 white doves and 20 cute kittens at a room temperature of precisely 75 degrees'.

Taylor Swift. The blurb says: 'a charming gourmand – floral with sparkling fruity tones on a woody background'.

What it should smell like: 'salty break-up tears'.

We might all like the idea of emulating the A-List by merely spraying some fragrant water on to our pulse points, but unfortunately it just isn't that easy. By the time we've realised all this, however, it's too late. We've already handed over our 25 quid.

A new age

It was 31 August 1997. Just a few weeks into my first job, I was awoken by the ringing of my new mobile phone, something bought for me by my parents as a present for becoming 'a proper journalist'. It was a sleepy Sunday morning but I got the sense before I even answered the call that I was not about to enjoy a lie-in.

'Holly, it's work,' came the voice down the line. 'You're going to need to come in. Princess Diana's been killed in a car crash.'

The blood drained from my face. I was still half asleep and a little hungover and wondered if I was hearing right. Princess Diana dead? I briefly wondered if this was some kind of test, an initiation from my new bosses to see if I could really cut it in the showbiz world. Switching on the TV to check, I immediately realised that it was no test.

I washed quickly, throwing on my clothes, and necked a few painkillers to recover from the night before. I poked my head into Erica's room on the way out.

'You might want to turn on the TV,' I whispered to her. She mumbled from under her duvet, an arm fumbling around aimlessly for the remote on the side table. A few seconds later, as I was closing the front door behind me, I heard a shout from inside the flat. 'Holy shit!' came my friend's voice. She'd obviously found the remote.

Sunday mornings in London are always strangely quiet but this one had an added layer of eeriness. What cars there were seemed to be driving more slowly, and on the underground my few fellow passengers looked shocked. Work, on the other hand, was noisy and buzzing, my new colleagues running around the office in their scruffy weekend clothes, everyone given specific tasks to help create a tribute issue of the mag. I was asked to come up with a list of Diana's most iconic dresses and to make sure we had the photos to back it up. When I got a job as a showbiz journalist, I had expected to be hanging out at rock festivals not worrying about the Royals. Wasn't that for tweedy middle-aged women and their tweedy middle-aged magazines? But looking back on the Princess's life that morning, it struck me how she had blurred the lines between the entertainment world and the monarchy like no one before her. She befriended pop stars and created trends – the world's most photographed woman. Here was no princess in the shadows. She was the biggest movie star of the eighties, without having ever made a movie.

The press's relationship with the monarchy has never been the same since that fateful day. In the wake of Diana's death the British Royal Family – well, the young and pretty ones at least – are showbiz fodder like never before, their profiles constantly compared to that of Di, the woman who started it all. And the public interest is sky high.

Yet at the same time a professional distance has to be kept, partly as a result of the feverish scrutiny Diana was forced to endure, attention which is sometimes blamed for her death. So while we can make the Duchess of Cambridge getting a new hairstyle into big news, we're also conscious of where to draw the line. It's what Princess Diana's brother, Earl Spencer, asked for in his speech at her funeral. Some scummier journalists still might not care, but I like to think the better ones show more respect.

It's a climate of compromise that allows for celebration of the Royals rather than a dissection of them. These people, unlike singers or movie stars, didn't choose to be in the public eye after all. They just have to deal with it the best they can. Reading about Diana's problematic relationship with the press during the week after her death certainly didn't make me wish I'd been doing my job ten years earlier. I was relieved to be starting my career at what seemed to be the commencement of a new age, albeit a tragically accidental one.

That Sunday it dawns on me that the world will continue to have an insatiable fascination with celebrity, but from now on we journalists will be under more inspection than ever. It's a hugely difficult balance to get right. Sure enough, in the decades after the death of Diana there have been various high-profile investigations into media practice and debates about our behaviour. The 'phone-hacking' revelations concerning the *News of the World* would eventually force Britain's most popular newspaper to shut down in 2011. The variety of questionable examples of journalism at the BBC, meanwhile – from sneakily editing the Queen in a TV trailer to Russell Brand naughtily goading a former sitcom star on the radio – became national scandals, resulting in hundreds of sackings and resignations.

We now have a 24-hour news culture where journalists are pushed harder for content than ever before – yet we're also under the microscope. It's no wonder I've so many colleagues who give it all up for an easier life.

So not only did I discover with the death of 'The People's Princess' that my new job might be more varied than I imagined and more emotional than a college course could ever prepare me for, I also discovered that specialising in the supposedly fluffy entertainment world would be no pushover. Journalism would require me to master being a tough mix of both ruthless and moral; a sniffer dog with ethics. Whether you're dealing with the tragic death of a global icon or the showy shallowness of a red carpet, that's no easy task.

Life is rarely like the movies. It doesn't usually have the tidy beginning, middle and end that we audiences demand from our films. Things are normally a lot more random and I for one have no idea how or when my professional life will draw to a close. (So, sorry folks . . . you'll find no neat walk off into the sunset in this story.)

Still, as I near the completion of this book, having spent many chapters looking back over incidents in my professional life, I can see that my time as a showbiz reporter did at least *begin* at an important time for the industry. Screenwriters dream of that kind of synchronicity when they're knocking out their scripts, but for me, it was unplanned.

Arriving home that Sunday night, exhausted and fragile, I find Erica still watching TV coverage of the day's events.

'Hey Holls. How's work?'

I'm fumbling around for an answer.

'To be honest,' I eventually reply, 'I really don't know yet. But I'm pretty sure about one thing. I've only been doing this job a few weeks but, after today, I know it will never be quite the same again.'

Epilogue

'Skank!'

I'm being called horrible names, but I don't mind. I've got Robert Pattinson next to me. Well, sort of – I've got a cardboard cut-out of Robert Pattinson next to me. (To those of you wondering how I could tell the difference, shame on you.)

It's a *Twilight* premiere and I'm getting Erica to take a picture of me standing next to a giant Edward model that's in the entrance to the party. I'm not ashamed. I've been swept up by the brooding romance of those stories for a few years now despite, like so many of the fans I'm sure, being long past my own tumultuous teenage years. If Stephenie Meyer had been writing when I grew up in the nineties, I'd definitely have been a 'Twihard', fiercely flaring up at anyone who dared to criticise Kristen or Rob. Had Twitter been around, there's no doubt my profile name would have been @ futuremrspattinson or a similarly confident declaration. It's why I knew I had to get tickets for tonight's premiere. While the film itself is hardly a barrel of laughs, we're having a great time at the after party: champagne, finger food and life-size mannequins of R Pattz to paw.

But a gaggle of young girls walking past us are shouting: 'You is way too old for him!'

Erica visibly bristles, looking as if she's about to go into Lara Croft mode (she does a kickboxing class every Wednesday). I hold her back, though. In fact I go even further. I burst out laughing.

'What's so funny? I could slap those little cows.'

'Bless 'em,' I giggle, watching the girls walk off into the party. 'I'm laughing cos . . . well . . . they're just like me.'

Okay, so it's a long time since I convinced myself that I would marry Mark Owen and that anyone else who felt the same thing deserved to die (I was a melodramatic young thing), but I still understand how passions can make you protective; how fandom can make you fierce. I still feel bad for the fellow Take That obsessive I shamelessly elbowed out of the way at one of the boys' gigs in 1995. If you're reading this and remember getting a bruised rib in Manchester during 'Never Forget', I'm sorry. If it's any consequence I have . . . ahem . . . *never forgotten*.

The internet now provides the cyber equivalent of elbows-to-the-chest, a breeding ground for catty comments, with the culprits hiding behind computer screens. It's a shame that fans who theoretically have like-minded views on an artist can get so worked up that some comments are little less than bullying. But put a load of fired-up teenage girls together in a space – whether online or in Manchester's Nynex Arena – and you don't have to be David Attenborough to predict the animal-like behaviour that will follow.

Still, when I'm in bed later that night – or, more accurately, early the next morning – I have a moment of uncertainty. Maybe I *am* too old for all this? After all, where are all the middle-aged showbiz reporters? You just don't see them. As the years go on I realise more and more that I'm the 'veteran', and my colleagues seem to be getting younger and younger, not to mention the stars I have to write about. At the moment I feel fine with doing the job I'm doing, but one day I may think about giving it up simply because I'll look so out of place.

Entertainment journalism, I've come to accept, is a young person's game. It's not just because of the odd hours, but because as we grow up we also start to see this line of work for what it is – fun, but ultimately silly. When we hit our thirties, pontificating on whether teen pop star A is dating teen pop star B starts to look less and less important. It's partly because our mortgages and our pensions and our love of fine bedding have all taken over as primary concerns. It's mainly, however, because we've seen it all before. There's very little that's truly new in showbiz; everything is cyclical. Even as we mourn the loss of an amazing talent, an Amy or a Whitney, gone before their time, we find ourselves thinking back to all the other occasions when we've written similar obituaries. At some point it seems that you can simply have enough showbiz in your life.

I'm not at that point yet – I'm still pathetically excited by having my photo taken next to a Rob Pattinson cut-out – but the evidence is all there in front of me. Several friends from this world have now moved out of London to start families, living lives both geographically and professionally hundreds of miles away from mine. I don't think they'll ever come back. The handful of straight boys that started out around the same time as me have played the game sensibly and risen up the ranks at their employer's, now more managers than news hounds. Even some of the gay men start to look out of place. A camp middle-aged man still flitting around parties and worrying about One Direction is just plain odd. And if you think those examples sound like gender stereotypes, then I'm not going to argue with you. I may be in the 'trendy London media' as my mum likes to call it, but you'd be surprised at how, when you look beyond the façade, things are as conservative as a seventies sitcom.

The thing is, whenever I waver and think about giving it all up, I find myself transported back to college, reliving the passion and drive I had back then for a world that so fascinated me. Reminiscing like that quickly reminds me that, really, I haven't changed. My outlets might be different – monthly glossies instead of student newspapers – but ultimately I'm still fascinated by our biggest stars for the same reason I always have been: pure admiration. I admire their drive, their talent, their showmanship – intoxicating ingredients found in almost every recipe for success. Fans will always remain essential to the showbiz world's existence and just because I've moved on from being a screaming 14-year–old, that doesn't mean I can't still be young and excitable at heart. For a showbiz journalist, being intrigued by the world of fame is essential – whatever your age.

I'm not married yet and I don't have children, but who knows? Maybe one day. Whatever happens, I just can't imagine myself not being energised by a cool new band, hot new film, or meeting an old-time icon with a story to tell. Fame is an endlessly complex business, ever worthy of investigation and discussion. If I can keep doing that, away from the hype and hot-air that has come to represent so much of my industry in the last few years, then I'll be happy even with wrinkles on my face.

It's another reason why I never sought fame myself. Away from public scrutiny I can hopefully carry on for as long as I get the results, rather than suffering from the whims of fashion so associated with being a celebrity. Over the last decade you've probably read one of my stories in a magazine or caught a glimpse of an interview that I did for a TV show and never even thought about where the story came from. Maybe I've even influenced you to download an album or watch a new drama? Quietly celebrating talented people and the work they do is what gives me a real buzz in this weird world that I work in. I hope you get a buzz from it too. Long may it continue.

I look at my bedside clock: 3.20 a.m. It's been a long old day . . . but I'm still not tired.

Pop quiz

So let's finish by seeing what showbiz knowledge you've got stored up there in your head, shall we? There are no prizes or anything – just the satisfaction that you are a Queen or a King of the entertainment world. No reading back issues of *Heat* to find out the answers though.

1. Name one of Brad and Angelina's kids (biological or adopted, I'm not fussy).

2. Jade Goody appeared on which series of *Big Brother*?

3. From which country does Justin Bieber originate?

4. Which person links John Mayer, Vince Vaughn and Justin Theroux?

5. Whose fragrances include 'Gold', 'Glam' and 'True Reflection'?

6. Who was the first winner of *The X Factor* back in 2004?

7. What is Adele's surname?

8. Who was the first Spice Girl to have a solo Number 1?

9. The Oscars currently takes place in which month?

10. Who designed Kate Middleton's wedding dress?

11. Name all five members of One Direction.

12. Whose autobiography was called *Through My Eyes*?

13. In what year did *EastEnders* start?

14. What are Ant & Dec's surnames?

15. Who is the famous husband of Ayda Field?

And the answers . . .

1. Maddox, Pax, Zahara, Shiloh, Knox, Vivienne.

2. The third series.

3. Canada.

4. Jennifer Aniston – she's dated all of them.

5. The kool and klassy Kim Kardashian.

6. Steve Brookstein. Remember him?

7. Adkins.

8. Mel B, with her song 'I Want You Back' from 1998.

9. February.

10. Sarah Burton, from Alexander McQueen.

11. Louis, Niall, Zayn, Harry and Liam. By the way, it's only okay to know that if you're either under 30 or a professional showbiz reporter.

12. Cheryl Cole. It's mainly pictures to be honest.

13. 1985.

14. McPartlin & Donnelly.

15. Robbie Williams.

Acknowledgements

Thanks to Rachel for her expert guidance – and our heated debates about Carrie Bradshaw!

Confessions of a Showbiz Reporter is part of the bestselling
'Confessions' series. Also available:

Confessions
of a
GP

The
Number
One
Bestseller

DR. BENJAMIN DANIELS

Confessions of a Male Nurse

MICHAEL ALEXANDER

Confessions
of a
New York
Taxi Driver

EUGENE SALOMON

Confessions
of a Police
Constable

MATT DELITO

Look out for *Confessions of an Undercover Cop* and *Further Confessions of a GP*, coming soon.